the **NO-NONSENSE** guide to
GLOBALIZATION
Wayne Ellwood

The No-Nonsense Guide to Globalization
First published in the UK by
New Internationalist Publications Ltd
Oxford OX4 1BW, UK
www.newint.org

in association with

Verso
6 Meard Street
London
W1F 0EG
www.versobooks.com

Cover photo: The Stock Market

Design by Andrew Kokotka/Ian Nixon, New Internationalist Publications Ltd.
Production editor: Troth Wells.

Printed by TJ International, Padstow, Cornwall, UK.

British Library Cataloguing in Publication Data.
A catalogue record for this book is available from the British Library.

Library of Congress Cataloguing-in-Publication Data.
A catalogue record for this book is available from the Library of Congress.

ISBN - 1 85984 336 0

the **NO-NONSENSE** guide to
GLOBALIZATION
Wayne Ellwood

VERSO

Foreword

THIS IS AN important work for anyone concerned about the future of planetary life. It is a clear and richly factual overview of the global corporate system – from its colonial past beginning with Cristóbal Colón's famous 1492 search for a sea route to the fabled riches of East Asia, to the current regime of 'globalization' in which a comprehensive plan to subordinate domestic economies everywhere to transnational banking and corporate rule is now into high gear.

Ceaseless repetition of slogans of 'inevitable change' and 'necessary restructuring' have everywhere accompanied this rapid prying-open of national economies and cultures for foreign exploitation 'free of trade and investment barriers'. But there is an astonishing gap between the dominant ideology of a 'self-regulating global free market' and the reality of tens of thousands of trade-lawyer constructed regulations imposed across the world by a fast-moving, secretive process instituting the private demands of transnational corporations as absolute rights to which elected legislatures everywhere are made subordinate.

The fact is that the very opposite of a 'free market' is at work. Since the fall of the Berlin Wall, corporate financial interests and their mass media vehicles have together stormed governments with an overwhelming agenda for world corporate rule. The rules are political, but unspoken. Either governments competitively enact this agenda, or deregulated capital and election funding will go elsewhere and resistant leaders will be ignored or pilloried in the corporate press.

The public is reassured that 'a rising tide of growth will lift all boats'. The demand is that 'global market competition be made free of the tax and regulatory burdens of government'. But the harsh reality is the very opposite of rising standards of living and new freedoms for the world's peoples. On almost every indicator of social and ecological life – from health protection, literacy development and future vocations for the young to maintenance of biodiversity and the planet's security of air, water, soil and climate – the restructuring of societies for corporate globalization has been increasingly life-destructive.

This book's wide-lensed and well-informed coverage of the system's global operations exposes the life-blind economics at work in a graphic explanation of what is really going on. If there is to be a turning of global governance towards true sustainability, we need to recognize that it has to be in a direction that makes civil and planetary life sovereign instead of instrumentalizing both for the money-to-more-money feeding cycle of transnational financial interests.

This policy itself, in turn, can only be achieved by people awakening in large numbers to the spectacularly failed program of corporate globalization. *The No-Nonsense Guide to Globalization* provides a lucid explanatory map of our current condition. For all who seek to think past corporate slogans to life-responsible government, this is a concise and valuable overview of the world system, what has gone wrong with it – and the way ahead.

Professor John McMurtry, *Department of Philosophy, University of Guelph, Ontario, Canada.*

the **NO-NONSENSE** guide to
GLOBALIZATION
Wayne Ellwood

CONTENTS

the NO-NONSENSE guide to
GLOBALIZATION

THERE IS LITTLE doubt that 'globalization' is the buzzword of the moment, the most talked-about and perhaps the least understood concept of this new millennium.

Environmentalists, human rights advocates, trade unionists, Third World farmers and citizens' groups decry it at meetings of the world's power élite in Seattle, Washington and Prague. At the same time economists and business journalists churn out shelves of hefty tomes praising 'globalization' as an 'historical inevitability'. But what does the term really mean? And how do we separate the reality from the propaganda?

Those are tough questions but they need answering. The entanglement of diverse cultures and economies now known as globalization has been spreading for centuries and the world has been shrinking as a result. In that sense it is an old story. Peppers, maize and potatoes, once found only in Latin America are now common foods in India, Africa and Europe. Spices originally from Indonesia thrive in the Caribbean. The descendants of African slaves, first brought to work the land of the 'new world,' have become Americans, Jamaicans, Canadians, Brazilians and Guyanese. American cotton, which helped usher in the first phase of the European industrial revolution, is farmed in Egypt and the Sudan.

But the 'old story' of globalization today has developed a new twist sparked by the rapid rate of technological change over the last 25 years. The micro-electronics revolution has irrevocably changed the essence of human contact on Earth. Distances are shrinking and information is spreading faster than ever before. The Internet and the World Wide Web have helped this process, enabling business to communicate more smoothly and efficiently and sparking what some have called the 'third wave' of economic growth.

At the same time these new channels of communication have helped spread a homogenous and largely commercial culture. Disney movies are children's fodder the world over. Barbie dolls, fast-food restaurants, hip-hop music and corporate-driven, American-style youth culture attract millions of new converts from the *bidonvilles* of Abidjan, Côte d'Ivoire, to the wealthy suburbs of Sydney. Alternatively you can now find a dazzling variety of 'ethnic' foods – including Thai, Szechwan, Mexican and Indian – throughout Europe, North America and Australia. In fact, many residents and visitors to Britain believe globalization and the resulting 'fusion' of cuisine is the best thing to happen to English cooking in the past 500 years.

There is every reason to believe this global exchange of people, products, plants, animals, technologies and ideas will continue into the future. The process of change is unstoppable. And that is not such a bad thing. In many ways it is a positive process containing the seeds of a better future for all the world's people. Globalization cannot help but be a positive force for change if we come to recognize the common thread of humanity that ties us together.

And change as we all know is inevitable. Humankind has always had a curiosity about the unknown and a passion to fully explore the world we inhabit. It is part of what makes us human. This restless spirit is what drives globalization and it is a seductive and powerful promise. For Westerners in particular it appeals to our deeply-seated beliefs in social and economic progress, fundamental human goals which are anchored in the liberal humanism of the Enlightenment.

We believe strongly that humankind can make the world a better place, both through improved technologies and a scientific understanding of the natural world. This is our destiny and for many of us it is our vocation. Economic progress is the one sure indicator of human development and the vision of a globally unified market is the logical route to that destination.

Economic globalization, the expansion of trade in goods and services between countries, is said to be the key to a more equal, more peaceful, less parochial world. For generations the received wisdom has been that the free market is the engine of human progress, based on the notion that open markets unleash the true potential of human society and are the threshold to the free play of ideas, the spread of universal human rights and the deep desire for democratic government. Eventually, so the argument goes, global integration and cross-cultural understanding will result in a borderless world where political parochialisms are put aside in a new pact of shared universal humanity.

These are compelling arguments partly because the promise of economic prosperity has not been without substance. We live in a world of fabulous wealth and opportunity. There are now more people living longer, healthier, more productive lives than at any time in human history. And much of that is due to the extraordinary capacity of industrial capitalism to produce the goods. The problem is that wealth creation has become the sine qua non of globalization. The social goals, the cohesive values that make us work as communities, are being ignored in the headlong rush to break down the barriers to global trade. Globalization has the potential to bring major improvements in productivity, innovation and creativity. But it is being overshadowed by a corporate-led plan for economic integration which threatens to undermine the whole project. Instead of helping build a better world for all, the current free-market model is eroding both democracy and equity.

Gaps between rich and poor are widening, decision-making power is concentrated in fewer and fewer hands, local cultures are wiped out, biological diversity is destroyed, regional tensions are increasing and the environment is nearing the point of collapse. That is the sad reality of globalization, an opportunity for human progress whose great potential has been thwarted. Instead we have a global economic system which feeds on itself while marginalizing the fundamental human needs of people and communities.

This *No-Nonsense Guide* sketches the picture of that global economic system – its history, its structure, its failings – and the forces in whose interest it works. By understanding how we got here and what is at stake perhaps we can find a route out of our current impasse. The solutions for transition and change are very much in process and I hint at some of these in the final chapter. But the hard facts are clear: unless we begin to alter the current global economic system, and soon, the tangible benefits of globalization will be swamped by a rising tide of inequality and injustice.

A final note. My focus here is the global economic system. So the text deals little with either cultural or political globalization, though there is a rich literature in both these areas. And either could easily form the basis of another book.

Wayne Ellwood
Toronto

1 Globalization then and now

Globalization is a new word which describes an old process: the integration of the global economy that began in earnest with the launch of the European colonial era five centuries ago. But the process has accelerated over the past quarter century with the explosion of computer technology, the dismantling of trade barriers and the expanding political and economic power of multinational corporations.

FIVE CENTURIES AGO, in a world without mobile phones, refrigeration, fax machines, automobiles, airplanes or nuclear weapons, one man had a foolish dream. Or so it seemed at the time. Cristóbal Colón, an ambitious young Genoese sailor and adventurer, was obsessed with Asia – a region about which he knew nothing, apart from unsubstantiated rumors of its colossal wealth. Such was the strength of his obsession (some say his greed) that he was able to convince the King and Queen of Spain to finance a voyage into the unknown across a dark, seemingly limitless expanse of water then known as the Ocean Sea. His goal: to find the Grand Khan of China and the gold which was reportedly there in profusion.

Centuries later Colón would become familiar to millions of school children as Christopher Columbus, the famous 'discoverer' of the Americas. In fact, the 'discovery' was more of an accident. The intrepid Columbus never did reach Asia, not even close. Instead, after five weeks at sea, he found himself sailing under a tropical sun into the turquoise waters of the Caribbean, making his landfall somewhere in the Bahamas, which he promptly named San Salvador (the Savior). The place clearly delighted Columbus' weary crew. They loaded up with fresh water and unusual foodstuffs. And they were befriended by the islands' indigenous population, the Taino.

'They are the best people in the world and above all the gentlest,' Columbus wrote in his journal. 'They very willingly showed my people where the water was, and they themselves carried the full barrels to the boat, and took great delight in pleasing us. They became so much our friends that it was a marvel.'[1]

Twenty years and several voyages later, most of the Taino were dead and the other indigenous peoples of the Caribbean were either enslaved or under attack. Globalization, even then, had moved quickly from an innocent process of cross-cultural exchange to a nasty scramble for wealth and power. As local populations died off from European diseases or were literally worked to death, thousands of European colonizers followed. Their desperate quest was for gold and silver. But the conversion of heathen souls to the Christian faith gave an added fillip to their plunder. Eventually European settlers colonized most of the new lands to the north and south of the Caribbean.

Columbus' adventure in the Americas was notable for many things, not least his single-minded concentration on extracting as much wealth as possible from the land and the people. But more importantly his voyages opened the door to 450 years of European colonialism. And it was this centuries-long imperial era that laid the groundwork for today's global economy.

Old globalization

Globalization, though it may be a new term, is an age-old process and one firmly rooted in the history of colonialism. One of Britain's most famous imperial spokesmen, Cecil Rhodes, put the case for colonialism succinctly in the 1890s. 'We must find new lands,' he said, 'from which we can easily obtain raw materials and at the same time exploit the cheap slave labor that is available from the natives of the colonies. The colonies [will] also provide a dumping ground for the surplus goods produced in our factories.'[2]

During the colonial era European nations spread

their rule across the globe. The British, French, Dutch, Spanish, Portuguese, Belgians, Germans, and later the Americans, took possession of most of what was later called the Third World – as well as Australia, New Zealand (Aotearoa) and North America. In some places (the Americas, Australia, New Zealand and southern Africa) they did so with the intent of establishing new lands for European settlement. Elsewhere (Africa and Asia) their interest was more in the spirit of Rhodes' vision: markets and plunder. From 1600-1800 incalculable riches were siphoned out of Latin America to become the chief source of finance for Europe's industrial revolution.

Global trade expanded rapidly during the colonial period as European powers sucked in raw materials from their new dominions: furs, timber and fish from Canada; slaves and gold from Africa; sugar, rum and fruits from the Caribbean; coffee, sugar, meat, gold and silver from Latin America; opium, tea and spices from Asia. Ships crisscrossed the oceans. Heading towards the colonies their holds were filled with settlers and manufactured goods; returning home the stout galleons and streamlined clippers bulged with coffee, copra and cocoa. By the 1860s and the 1870s world trade was booming. It was a 'golden era' of international commerce – though the European powers pretty much stacked things in their favor. Wealth from their overseas colonies flooded into France, England, Holland and Spain but some of it also flowed back into the colonies as investment – into railways, roads, ports, dams and cities. Such was the extent of globalization a century ago that capital transfers from North to South were actually greater at the end of the 1890s than at the end of the 1990s. By 1913 exports (one of the hallmarks of increasing economic integration) accounted for a larger share of global production than they did in 1999.

When people talk about globalization today they're still talking mostly about economics, about an expanding international trade in goods and services based on

Tyranny and poverty

Colonialism in the Americas separated Indians from their land, destroyed traditional economies and left native people among the poorest of the poor.

- The Spanish ran the Bolivian silver mines with a slave labor system known as the *mita*; nearly eight million Indians had died in the Potosí mines by 1650.
- Suicide and alcoholism are common responses to social dislocation. Suicide rates on Canadian Indian reserves are 10 to 20 times higher than the national average.
- In Guatemala life expectancy for non-natives is 61 years; for Indians it is 45. The infant mortality rate for Indian children is twice that of non-Indians (160 deaths per thousand versus 80). ■

Indian Population of the Americas: 1492 and 1992

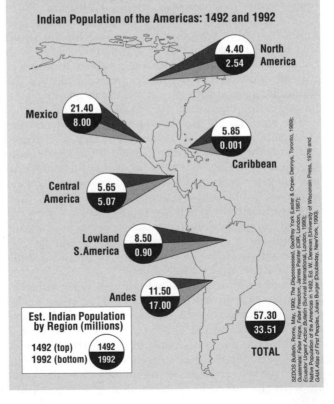

North America
4.40
2.54

Mexico
21.40
8.00

Caribbean
5.85
0.001

Central America
5.65
5.07

Lowland S.America
8.50
0.90

Andes
11.50
17.00

Est. Indian Population by Region (millions)
1492 (top)
1992 (bottom)
1492
1992

TOTAL
57.30
33.51

SEDOS Bulletin, Rome, May, 1990; The Dispossessed, Geoffrey York (Lester & Orpen Dennys, Toronto, 1989); Guatemala: False Hope, False Freedom, James Painter (CIIR, London, 1987); Ecuador Urgent Action Bulletin (Survival International, London, 1990); Native Population of the Americas in 1492, Ed. W. Denevan (University of Wisconsin Press, 1976) and GAIA Atlas of First Peoples, Julian Burger (Doubleday, New York, 1990).

the concept of 'comparative advantage'. This theory was first developed in 1817 by the British economist David Ricardo in his *Principles of Political Economy, and Taxation.* Ricardo wrote that nations should specialize in producing goods in which they have a natural advantage and thereby find their market niche. He believed this would benefit both buyer and seller but only if certain conditions were maintained, such as: 1) that trade between partners must be balanced so that one country doesn't become indebted and dependent on another; and 2) that investment capital must be anchored locally and not allowed to flow from a high-wage country to a low-wage country. Unfortunately, in today's high-tech world of instant communications neither of these key conditions exist, with the result that Ricardo's vision of local self-reliance mixed with balanced exports and imports is nowhere to be seen. Instead export-led trade has come to dominate the economic agenda with the only route to growth based on increasing exports to the rest of the world.

The rationale is that all countries and all peoples eventually benefit from the results of increased trade. And world trade has zoomed ahead in the last decade. It grew at an average 6.6 per cent during the 1990s and is set to grow at around 6 per cent a year over the next ten years. Global trade is actually growing faster than total world output which saw increases of 3.2 per cent during the 1990s and may reach 3 per cent annually over the next decade. This expansion of trade is expected to increase global income by up to $500 billion early in this new millennium.

Nonetheless, today's globalization is vastly different from the globalization of 50 or 100 years ago. The world has changed in the last century in ways that have completely altered the character of the global economy and its impact on people and the natural world. Even arch-capitalists like currency speculator George Soros have voiced doubts about the negative values that underlie the direction of the modern global economy.

'Insofar as there is a dominant belief in our society today,' he writes, 'it is a belief in the magic of the marketplace. The doctrine of *laissez-faire* capitalism holds that the common good is best served by the uninhibited pursuit of self-interest... Unsure of what they stand for, people increasingly rely on money as the criterion of value... The cult of success has replaced a belief in principles. Society has lost its anchor.'

Market magic

The 'magic of the marketplace' is not a new concept. It's been around in one form or another since the father of modern economics, Adam Smith, first published his pioneering work *The Wealth of Nations* nearly 250 years ago. But Smith's concept of the market was a far cry from the one touted by today's globalization cheerleaders. Smith was adamant that markets worked most efficiently when there was equality between buyers and sellers and when neither buyer nor seller was large enough to influence the market price. This, he said, would ensure that all parties involved got a fair return and that society as a whole would benefit through the best use of its natural and human resources. Smith also believed that capital was best invested locally so that owners could see what was happening with their investment and could have hands-on management of its use. Author and activist David Korten sums up Smith's thinking as follows:

'His vision of an efficient market was one composed of small owner-managed enterprises located in the communities where the owners resided. Such owners would share in the community's values and have a personal stake in its future. It is a market that has little in common with a globalized economy dominated by massive corporations without local or national allegiance, managed by professionals who are removed from real owners by layers of investment institutions and holding companies.' [3]

As Korten hints, the world we live in today is vastly

different from the one that Adam Smith inhabited. The first important change has been the communications technology revolution of the last 25 years. Computers, fiber-optics, satellites and the miniaturization of electronics have radically altered the production, sales and distribution of goods and services as well as the patterns of global investment. Coupled with improvements in air freight and cheap ocean transport, companies now tend to move their plants and factories wherever costs are lowest. Improved technology and cheap oil has led to a massive increase in goods being transported by air and sea. According to the Boeing Aircraft company, world air traffic cargo tripled from 1985 to 1997 and is predicted to triple again by 2015. The global shipping business which now consumes more than 140 million tons of fuel oil a year is expected to increase by 85 per cent in the next decade. And costs are falling too. Ocean freight unit costs have fallen by 70 per cent since the 1980s while air freight costs have fallen three to four per cent a year

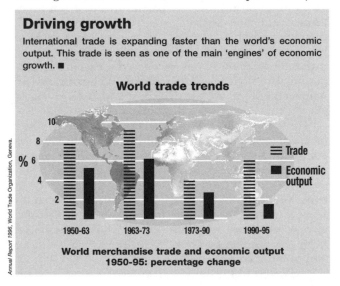

Driving growth

International trade is expanding faster than the world's economic output. This trade is seen as one of the main 'engines' of economic growth. ■

World trade trends

≡ Trade
■ Economic output

World merchandise trade and economic output 1950-95: percentage change

Annual Report 1996, World Trade Organization, Geneva.

on average over the last two decades.

These cheap transport rates in reality are 'cheap' only in a purely financial sense. They reflect 'internal' costs – the costs of production, packaging, marketing, labor, debt and profit. But they don't reflect at all the 'external' environmental impact of this accelerated use of fossil fuels. Moving more goods around the planet increases pollution and contributes to carbon dioxide in the atmosphere, a major source of global warming and climate change. These environmental costs are basically ignored by business. This is one of the main reasons environmentalists object to the globalization of trade. Companies make the profits, they complain, but society has to pay the bill.

The other key reason why globalization today is so different has to do with structural changes to the global economy that have occurred since the early 1970s. It was then that the system of rules set up at the end of World War Two to manage global trade collapsed. The fixed currency-exchange regime agreed at Bretton Woods in 1944 gave the world 25 years of more or less steady economic growth.

But around 1980 things began to change with the emergence of fundamentalist free-market governments in Britain and the US and the later disintegration of the state-run command economy in the former Soviet Union. The formula for economic progress adopted by the administrations of Margaret Thatcher in the UK and Ronald Reagan in the US called for a drastic reduction in the regulatory role of the state. Instead, government was to take a back seat to corporate executives and money managers. The overall philosophy was that companies must be free to move their operations anywhere in the world to minimize costs and maximize returns to investors. Free trade, unfettered investment, deregulation, balanced budgets, low inflation and privatization of publicly-owned enterprises were trumpeted as the six-step plan to national prosperity.

Hand-in-hand with the spread of free trade in goods and services came the deregulation of world financial markets. Banks, insurance companies and investment dealers which had been confined within national borders were suddenly unleashed. Within a few years the big players from Europe, Japan and North America expanded into each other's markets as well as into the newly-opened and fragile financial services markets in the South. Aided by computer technology and welcoming governments, the big banks and investment houses were keen to invest surplus cash in anything that would turn a quick profit. In this new relaxed atmosphere finance capital became a profoundly destabilizing influence on the global economy.

Instead of long-term investment in the production of real goods and services, speculators make money from money, with little concern for the impact of their investments on local communities or national economies. Governments everywhere now fear the destabilizing impact of this global financial casino. Recent United Nations (UN) studies show a direct correlation between the frequency of financial crises and the increase in international capital flows during the 1990s.

The collapse of the East Asian currencies which

Pinball capital

Short-term speculative capital whizzes around the world leaving ravaged economies and human devastation in its wake. East Asia (Indonesia, South Korea, Thailand, Malaysia, the Philippines) suffered a destructive net reversal of private capital flows from 1996 to 1997 of $12 billion. ■

Percentage change in GDP before and after the Asian financial crisis

	Thailand	Indonesia	Malaysia	S. Korea
Average 1980-90	7.6	6.1	5.2	9.4
Average 1990-96	8.3	7.7	8.7	7.3
Average 1997	-7	-16	-6	-5

Human Development Report 1999, UN Development Program / Oxford University Press; Financial Frenzy, Liberalization, Speculation and Regulation, War on Want, London 1999.

began in July 1997 is the most catastrophic recent example of the damage caused by nervous short-term investors. Until then the 'Tiger Economies' of Thailand, Taiwan, Singapore, Malaysia and South Korea had been the success stories of globalization. Advocates of free market growth pointed to these countries as proof that classic capitalism would bring wealth and prosperity to millions in the developing world – though they conveniently ignored the fact that in all these countries the State took a strong and active role in shaping the economy.

Foreign investment was tightly controlled by national governments until the early 1990s, severely in the case of South Korea and Taiwan, less so in Thailand and Malaysia. Then as a result of continued pressure from the International Monetary Fund (IMF) and others, the 'tigers' began to open up their capital accounts and private sector businesses began to borrow heavily.

Spectacular growth rates floated on a sea of foreign investment as offshore investors poured dollars into the region, eager to harvest double-digit returns. In 1996 capital was flowing into East Asia at almost $100 billion a year. But mostly the cash went into risky real estate ventures or onto the local stock market where it

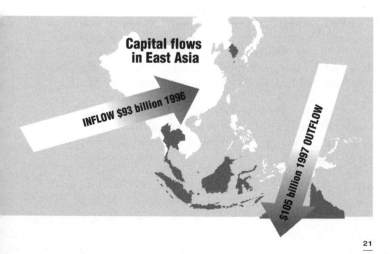

Capital flows in East Asia

INFLOW $93 billion 1996

$105 billion 1997 OUTFLOW

inflated share prices far beyond the value of their underlying assets.

In Thailand, where the Asian 'miracle' first began to sour, over-investment in real estate left the market glutted with $20 billion worth of new unsold properties. Then the house of cards collapsed. Foreign investors began to realize that the Thai financial institutions to which they had lent billions could not meet their loan repayments. Spooked by the specter of falling returns and a stagnant real estate market, investors at first slowly, and then in a panic-stricken rush, called in their loans and cashed in their investments.

More than $105 billion left the entire region in the next 12 months, equivalent to 11 per cent of the domestic output of the most seriously affected countries – Indonesia, the Philippines, South Korea, Thailand and Malaysia.[4] Having abandoned any kind of capital controls, Asian governments were powerless to stop the massive hemorrhage of funds. Ironically the IMF's 1997 *Annual Report*, written just before the crisis, had singled out Thailand's 'remarkable economic performance' and 'consistent record of sound macroeconomic policies'.

The IMF was to be proven wrong – disastrously so. The human costs of the East Asian economic crisis were immediate and devastating. As bankruptcies soared, firms shut their doors and millions of workers were laid off. More than 400 Malaysian companies declared bankruptcy between July 1997 and March 1998 while in Indonesia – the poorest country affected by the crisis – 20 per cent of the population or nearly 40 million people were pushed into poverty. And the impact of the economic slowdown had the devastating effect of reducing both family income and government expenditures on social and health services for years afterwards. In Thailand, more than 100,000 children were yanked from school when parents could no longer cough up tuition fees. The crash also had a knock-on effect outside Asia. Shock-waves rippled

Third World

If there's a Third World, then there must be a First and Second World too. When the term was first coined in 1952 by the French demographer, Alfred Sauvy, there was a clear distinction, though the differences have become blurred over the past decade. Derived from the French phrase, *tiers monde*, the term was first used to suggest parallels between the *tiers monde* (the world of the poor countries) and the *tiers état* (the third estate or common people of the French revolutionary era). The First World was the North American/European 'Western bloc' while the Soviet-led 'Eastern bloc' was the Second World. These two groups had most of the economic and military power and faced off in a tense ideological confrontation commonly called the 'Cold War'. Third World countries in Africa, Latin America, Asia and the Pacific had just broken free of colonial rule and were attempting to make their own way rather than become entangled in the tug-of-war between East and West. Since the break-up of the Soviet Union in the early 1990s the term Third World has less meaning and its use is diminishing. Now many refer to the 'developing nations', the Majority World or just the South. ■

through Latin America, nearly tipping Brazil into recession while the Russian economy suffered worse damage. Growth rates slipped into reverse and the Russian ruble became nearly worthless as a medium of international exchange.

The East Asian economic crisis was a serious blow to the 'promise' of economic globalization. It was the first time that the 'global managers' and finance kingpins showed that the system wasn't all it was made out to be. The global economy was more fragile, and thus more explosive, than anybody had imagined. As the region slowly recovered, more citizens around the world began to scratch their heads and wonder about the pros and cons of globalization. The mass public protests in Seattle (1999) and Prague (2000) were still to come. But the East Asian crisis planted real seeds of doubt about the merits of corporate globalization.

1 *The Conquest of Paradise: Christopher Columbus and the Columban Legacy*, Kirkpatrick Sale, Knopf, New York 1990. **2** *The Ecologist*, Vol 29, No 3, May/June 1999. **3** *When Corporations Rule the World*, David Korten, Kumarian/Berrett-Koehler, West Hartford/San Francisco, 1995. **4** *Human Development Report 1999*, United Nations Development Program, New York/Oxford, 1999.

2 The Bretton Woods Trio

**The Great Depression of the 1930s leads to the birth
of Keynesianism and the interventionist state. As
World War Two ends, the victors put together a new
set of rules for the global economy. This postwar
financial architecture includes the World Bank, the
International Monetary Fund (IMF) and the General
Agreement on Tariffs and Trade (GATT). But as Third
World nations emerge from centuries of colonialism
these institutions are seen increasingly as pillars of
the status quo.**

AS WORLD WAR TWO was drawing to a close, the
world's leading politicians and government officials,
mostly from the victorious 'Allied' nations (Britain,
Canada, Australia, New Zealand and the United
States) began to think about the need to establish a
system of rules to run the postwar global economy.

Before the widespread outbreak of the war in 1939
trading nations everywhere had been racked by a crip-
pling economic depression. When the US stock market
crashed in 1929 nations turned inward in an attempt to
pull themselves out of the steep skid. But without a system of global rules there was no coherence or larger
logic to the 'beggar-thy-neighbor' polices adopted
worldwide. High tariff barriers were thrown up between
countries with the result that world trade nose-dived,
economic growth spluttered and mass unemployment
and poverty followed. As a result the 1930s became a
decade of radical politics and rancorous social ferment
in the West as criticism of laissez-faire capitalism and an
unchecked market economy grew.

Scholars like Karl Polanyi helped to reinforce a
growing suspicion of a market-based economic model
which put money and investors at the center of its
concerns rather than social values and human well-
being. 'To allow the market mechanism to be the sole

director of the fate of human beings and their natural environment... would result in the demolition of society,' Polanyi wrote in his masterwork, *The Great Transformation.*

Polanyi was not alone in his distrust of the market economy. Other thinkers like the influential Cambridge-educated economist John Maynard Keynes were also grappling with a way of controlling global markets, making them work for people and not the other way around. Keynes both admired and feared the power of the market system. With the memory of the Great Depression of the 1930s still fresh in his mind he predicted that, without firm boundaries and controls, capitalism would be immobilized by its own greed, and would eventually self-destruct. As it happened only World War Two turned things around. The War set the factories and farms humming again as millions of troops were deployed by all sides in the conflict. Armaments manufacturers, aircraft factories and other military suppliers ran 24-hour shifts. Years later, as the war wound down, government policy makers began to think about how to ensure a smooth transformation to a peacetime economy.

It was Keynes' radical notion of an 'interventionist' state to which governments turned in an effort to set their economies back on a steady keel. Until the worldwide slump of the 1930s the accepted economic wisdom had been that unemployment was a 'normal condition' of the free market. The economy might go up and down according to the normal business cycle but in the long run, growth (and increased global trade) would create new jobs and sop up the unemployed.

Keynes was skeptical of this orthodoxy, suggesting that the economy was a human-made artifact and that people acting together through their government could have some control over its direction. Why not act now, he suggested, since 'in the long run we're all dead.' His approach offered a way out for governments who found themselves helplessly mired in economic stagnation.

In *The General Theory of Employment, Interest and Money* published in 1936, Keynes argued that the free market, left on its own, actually creates unemployment. Profitability, he said, depends on suppressing wages and cutting costs by replacing labor with technology. In other words profits and a certain amount of unemployment go hand-in-hand. So far so good, at least for those making the profits. But then Keynes showed that lowering wages and laying off workers would inevitably result in fewer people who could afford to buy the goods that factories were producing. As demand fell, so would sales, and factory owners would be forced to lay off even more workers. This, reasoned Keynes, was the start of a downward spiral with terrible human consequences.

To 'prime the economic pump' Keynes suggested governments intervene actively in the economy. He reasoned that business owners and rich investors are unlikely to open their wallets if the prospects for growth look dim. When the economy is in a tailspin then it is up to government to step in – by spending on public goods like education, health care, job training, roads, dams, trams and railways. And by wading in with direct financial support to the unemployed.

Even if governments had to go into debt to kick-start economic growth Keynes advised politicians not to worry. The price was worth it. By directly stimulating the economy, government could rekindle demand and help reverse the downward spiral. Soon companies would begin to invest again to increase production to meet the growing demand. This would mean hiring more workers with more money in their pockets. As jobs increased so would taxes. Eventually, the government would be able to pay back its debt from increased tax revenues raised from a now healthy, growing economy.

Desperate Western governments were quick to adopt the 'Keynesian' solution to economic stagnation. In the US the 'New Deal' policies of the Roosevelt administration were directly influenced by Keynes. The American Employment Act of 1946 accepted the federal government's responsibility 'to promote maximum employment, production and purchasing power'. The British Government, too, in 1944 accepted as one of its primary aims 'the maintenance of a high and stable level of employment after the war.'

Other countries like Canada, Australia and Sweden quickly followed. Keynes' influence spread and people began to believe that economics was finally a manageable science in the service of human progress.

'We are witnessing a development under which the economic system ceases to lay down the law to society and the primacy of society over that system is secured.' Thus wrote Polanyi in a moment of supreme optimism just before the end of the war.

Bretton Woods

It was this assurance and confidence that delegates from 44 nations brought to the postcard-pretty New England resort village of Bretton Woods in July 1944. The aim of the Bretton Woods Conference was to erect a new framework for the postwar global economy – a stable, cooperative international monetary system which would promote national sovereignty and prevent future financial crises. The purpose was not to bury capitalism but to save it. The main proposal was for a system of fixed exchange rates. In the light of the depression of the previous decade floating rates were now seen as inherently unstable and destructive of national development plans.

Keynes' influence at Bretton Woods was significant. But despite his lobbying and cajoling he did not win the day on every issue. In the end the huge military and economic clout of the Americans proved impossible to overcome.

The Conference rejected his proposals to establish a world 'reserve currency' administered by a global central bank. Keynes believed this would have created a more stable and fairer world economy by automatically recycling trade surpluses to finance trade deficits. However his solution did not fit the interests of the United States, eager to take on the role of the world's economic powerhouse. Instead the Conference opted for a system based on the free movement of goods with the American dollar as the international currency. The dollar was linked to gold and the price of gold was fixed at $35 an ounce (28g). In effect the US dollar became 'as-good-as-gold' and in this one act became the dominant currency of international exchange.

Three governing institutions emerged from the gathering to oversee and coordinate the global economy. These were not neutral economic mechanisms: they contained a powerful bias in favor of global competition and corporate enterprise. And each had a distinct role to play:

1 THE INTERNATIONAL MONETARY FUND (IMF)

The IMF was born with a mission: to create economic stability for a world which had just been through the trauma of depression and the devastation of war. As originally conceived it was supposed to 'facilitate the expansion and balanced growth of international trade' and 'to contribute to the promotion and maintenance of high levels of employment and real income'.

A major part of its job was to oversee a system of 'fixed' exchange rates. This was supposed to stop countries from devaluing their national currencies to get a competitive edge over their neighbors – a defining feature of the economic chaos of the 1930s.

Another part of the Fund's mandate was to promote currency 'convertibility' – to make it easier to exchange one currency for another when trading across national borders and in this way to encourage world trade.

And finally the new agency was to act as a 'lender-of-last-resort' supplying emergency loans to countries which ran into short-term cash flow problems. Keynes' idea was to set up an International Clearing Union which would automatically provide unconditional loans to countries experiencing balance-of-payments problems. These loans would be issued 'no strings attached' and their purpose would be to support domestic demand and maintain employment. Otherwise countries feeling the pinch would be forced to balance their deficit by cutting off imports and smothering their domestic economy.

Keynes argued that international trade was a two-way street and that the 'winners' (those countries in surplus) were as obligated as the 'losers' (those countries in deficit) to bring the system back into balance. In fact, Keynes suggested that pressure be brought to bear on surplus nations so they would be forced to increase their imports and recycle the surplus to deficit nations.

But Keynes' view did not prevail. Instead a proposal put forward by US Treasury Secretary Harry Dexter White became the basis for the IMF. The International Clearing Union idea disappeared. IMF members would not automatically receive loans when they tumbled into deficit. Instead members would have access to limited loan amounts which were to be determined by a complex quota system.

When a country joins the IMF it is assigned a quota which is calculated in Special Drawing Rights (SDRs), the Fund's own unit of account. Quotas are assigned according to a country's relative position in the world economy which means that the most powerful economies have the most influence and clout. The US for example has the largest SDR quota at about 27 billion. The size of a member's quota determines a lot, including how many votes it has in IMF deliberations and how much foreign exchange it has access to if it runs into choppy financial waters.

Balance-of-payments loans are at less than the prevailing rate and members are supposed to use and repay them within five years. The issue of whether the IMF could attach conditions to these loans was lost in the verbiage of the original Bretton Woods agreement. But Harry Dexter White was very clear six months later when he wrote in the journal *Foreign Affairs* that the Fund would not simply dole out money to debtor countries. The IMF would force countries to take measures which under the old gold standard (see p34) would have happened automatically.

While the framers of the Bretton Woods agreements supported a gradual reduction of trade barriers and tariffs they were less enthusiastic about allowing the free movement of capital internationally.

Keynes, Britain's delegate to the meeting, advocated a balanced world trade system with strict controls on the movement of capital across borders. He held that the free movement of all goods and capital, advocated most powerfully by the US delegation, would inevitably lead to inequalities and instabilities.

2 THE WORLD BANK (INTERNATIONAL BANK FOR RECONSTRUCTION AND DEVELOPMENT)

One of the other key goals of the Bretton Woods Conference was to find a way to rebuild the economies of those nations that had been devastated by World War Two. The International Bank for Reconstruction and Development (IBRD) was created to spearhead this effort. The Bank is funded by dues from its members and by money borrowed on international capital markets. It makes loans to members below rates available at commercial banks. Its initial mandate was to provide loans for economic 'infrastructure' which included things like power plants, dams, roads, airports, ports, agricultural development and education systems. The Bank poured money into reconstruction and development in Europe after World War Two. But it was not enough and it was not fast enough to satisfy the United States whose booming industries were in need of viable markets. In response the US set up its own, much looser, Marshall Plan which directly provided dollars to European nations, largely in the form of grants rather than loans.

As Europe gradually recovered in the 1950s the IBRD turned its interest to the newly-independent countries of the Third World where it became widely known as the World Bank. As Southern countries sought to enter the industrial age the Bank became a major player throughout the region. According to the 'stages of growth' economic theory popular at the time, developing nations could achieve economic 'take-off' only from a strong infrastructure 'runway'. It was part of the Bank's self-defined role to build this 'infrastructural capacity' and this it did enthusiastically by funding hydroelectric projects and highway systems throughout Latin America, Asia and Africa.

But despite the Bank's concessional lending rates it was clear early on that the very poorest countries would have difficulty meeting loan repayments. So in the late 1950s the Bank was pressured into setting up the International Development Association (IDA). This wing of the Bank was to provide 'soft loans' with very low interest or none at all – and so head off attempts by the new countries of the Third World to set up an independent funding agency separate from the Bretton Woods institutions which could operate under UN auspices. The Bank also established two other departments: the International Finance Corporation, which supports private-sector investment in Bank-approved projects, and the Multilateral Insurance Guarantee Agency, which provides risk insurance to foreign corporations and individuals who decide to invest in one of the Bank's member countries.

3 GENERAL AGREEMENT ON TARIFFS AND TRADE (GATT)/WORLD TRADE ORGANIZATION (WTO)

The GATT established a set of rules to govern global trade. Its aim was to reduce national trade barriers and to stop the competitive trade policies that had so hobbled the global economy prior to World War Two. Seven rounds of tariff reductions were negotiated under the GATT treaty – the final 'Uruguay Round' began in 1986.

In March 1994, following completion of the final round of talks, politicians and bureaucrats gathered in Marrakech, Morocco, to approve a new World Trade Organization (WTO) which was to replace the more loosely-structured GATT. The WTO, unlike the GATT, has the official status of an international organization rather than a loosely-structured treaty. It has 137 member states and 30 'observers' and vastly expands GATT's mandate in new directions. The text of the WTO agreement had 26,000 pages: its sheer physical size is a hint of both its prolixity and its complexity. It includes the GATT agreements which mostly focus on trade in goods. But it also folds in the new General Agreement on Trade in Services (GATS) which potentially affects more than 160 areas including telecommunications, banking and investment, transport, education, health and the environment.

From the outset GATT was seen as a 'rich man's club' dominated by Western industrial nations which were slow to concede their position of power. The WTO continues this tradition of rich world domination. Rubens Ricupero, current Secretary-General of the UN Conference on Trade and Development (UNCTAD) is frank in his assessment of the multilateral trading system. It is a matter of 'concrete evidence' he says that global trade rules are 'highly imbalanced and biased against developing countries'. Why is it, Ricupero asks, that developed countries have been given decades to 'adjust' their economies to imports of agricultural products and textiles from the Third World when poor countries are pressured to open their borders immediately to Western banks and telecommunication companies?

As a case in point he mentions the multifiber arrangement (MFA) on textiles under which industrial countries are allowed to impose quotas restricting clothing and textile imports from developing nations. The MFA developed from a waiver which the US demanded on behalf of its domestic cotton industry in the late 1950s. By the time the MFA is dismantled Ricupero notes it will already have lasted 50 years, a long time for a 'temporary' concession which was to allow US producers to adjust to cheap textile imports from abroad. [1]

In contrast, according to the UN Development Program (UNDP), developing countries have been much more willing to abandon once-popular import substitution policies and reduce trade barriers. India, for example, reduced its tariffs from an average of 82 per cent in 1990 to 30 per cent in 1997. Brazil chopped average tariffs from 25 per cent to 12 per cent over the same period and China lowered them from 43 per cent in 1993 to 18 per cent four years later.

The WTO pursues its free trade agenda with the single-minded concentration of the true believer. Nonetheless there is a growing unease about the organization's globalizing agenda. Critics are especially wary of the new Dispute Settlement Body (DSB) which

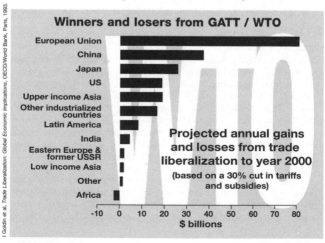

I Goldin et al, Trade Liberalization: Global Economic Implications, OECD/World Bank, Paris, 1993.

Winners and losers from GATT / WTO

- European Union
- China
- Japan
- US
- Upper income Asia
- Other industrialized countries
- Latin America
- India
- Eastern Europe & former USSR
- Low income Asia
- Other
- Africa

Projected annual gains and losses from trade liberalization to year 2000

(based on a 30% cut in tariffs and subsidies)

-10   0   10   20   30   40   50   60   70   80
$ billions

gives the WTO the legal tools to approve tough trade sanctions by one member against another, especially on nations which might disagree with the organization's interpretation of global trade rules. Any member country, acting on behalf of a business with an axe to grind, can challenge the laws and regulations of another country on the grounds that they violate WTO rules.

It used to be that if the GATT wanted to discipline one of its members for not playing according to the rules, every member had to agree. The WTO has considerably more power. The dispute settlement panel is comprised of appointed 'experts' who hear the case behind closed doors. If the DSB decides on sanctions the only way to escape them is if every member opposes them – a virtual impossibility. In effect the WTO regime is one of trade *über alles*. Environmental laws,

The gold standard

Until the Great Depression of the 1930s gold was the one precious metal that most large trading countries in the world recognized and accepted as a universal medium of exchange. The shift to gold began when international trade exploded after the industrial revolution. Britain was the first to adopt the gold standard in 1816; the US made the change in 1873 and by 1900 most of the world had joined them.

Most national currencies were redeemable in gold. Paper bank notes often contained the phrase 'the bank promises to pay the bearer on demand' the equivalent in gold. That implied you could go into a bank and demand the equivalent in gold if the mood moved you.

What that meant was that all nations set the value of their national currency in terms of ounces of gold (1 ounce = 28g). It was a convenient way of settling national trading accounts. And the fixed gold standard was supposed to both stabilize foreign exchange rates and domestic economies. A country's wealth could be measured by the amount of gold it had stored in its vaults; certainly an unfair advantage for those countries lucky enough to be sitting on vast natural deposits of gold.

With gold as a fixed standard the fluctuations of international trade were relatively simple to track. If a country's imports exceeded its exports then gold had to be shipped to those countries who were owed in order to balance the books. The decline in the amount of gold would labor standards, human rights legislation, public health policies, cultural protection, food self-reliance or any other policies held to be in the 'national interest' can be attacked as unfair 'impediments' to free trade.

Already there have been some cases where the WTO has effectively struck down national legislation in its pursuit of a 'level playing field'. The recent WTO decision against the European Union (EU) over the importing of bananas is a case in point. The WTO's 'most favored nation' clause demands that similar products from different member countries be treated equally. Under the terms of the Lomé Convention (agreement) the EU had promised to give preference to bananas from former European colonies in Africa, the Caribbean and the Pacific. In general these banana growers tend to be small farmers who are less dependent on pesticide-intensive plantation methods than the

then force a government to reduce the amount of cash in circulation. Because money was redeemable for gold both governments and banks would want to make sure they could cover themselves if necessary. Less money in circulation would tend to lower prices, dampening economic activity at home and decreasing imports. Gold flowing to countries on the receiving end would have the opposite effect. Governments would release more cash into the economy to cover the increase of gold in their vaults and prices would tend to increase.

With the Depression of the 1930s one country after another abandoned the gold standard in an attempt to 'devalue' their currencies to gain a 'competitive advantage' over their trading partners (i.e. to make their exports cheaper). There was an attempt to modify the gold link after World War Two when the US set the value of the dollar at $1/35$ an ounce (0.9g) of gold but holders of cash were no longer able to demand gold in exchange and the circulation of gold coins was prohibited. Then in 1973 US President Richard Nixon suspended the exchange of American gold for foreign-held dollars at fixed rates. At that point gold became just another commodity, its price determined by the law of supply and demand. Many countries (as well as the International Monetary Fund) continue to hold vast gold reserves and quantities are occasionally sold on the open market – though sellers are careful not to flood the market and depress the international price too much. ■

giant US companies like Dole and Chiquita.

The Europeans stressed that this was a matter of sovereign foreign policy in relation to former colonies while the US argued that EU tariffs prohibited American banana companies in Central America from reaching lucrative markets in Europe. The WTO decided on behalf of the US, ruling that the European preference was unfair. Meanwhile, small island nations in the Caribbean, so dependent on income from the banana trade, are worried the decision will cut off a guaranteed market and destroy their industry.

All nations have the right to use the DSB to pursue their own economic self-interest. But the fact is that the world's major trading nations are also its most powerful economic actors and so the tendency is for the strong to use the new rules to dominate weaker countries.

The 'national treatment clause' basically says that a country may not discriminate against products of foreign origin on any grounds whatsoever. And in so doing it removes the power of national governments to develop economic policy which serves the moral, ethical or economic interests of their citizenry. For example, if goods are produced by children in sweatshop conditions that doesn't enter the equation. And the same is true if a foreign factory fouls the air and poisons the water, if poverty wages are paid to the workers who produce the stuff, or if the goods themselves are poisonous and dangerous.

According to WTO rules any country that refuses to import a product on the grounds that it may harm public health or damage the environment has to prove the case scientifically. So Canada, the world's biggest asbestos producer, has petitioned the WTO's dispute panel to force the European Community to import the known carcinogen once again. And when the European Union (EU) refused imports of hormone-fed beef from North America, the US took the case to the WTO arguing that there was no threat to human health from cows fed hormones. The EU ban on hormone-fed beef applied to their own farmers as well as foreign producers but that made little difference. The WTO panel decided in favor of the US, effectively ruling that Europeans had no right to pass laws that supported their opposition to hormones. The EU was ordered to compensate producers in the US and Canada for every year of lost export earnings. And in retaliation the US imposed 100 per cent tariffs on a range of European imports including mustard, pork, truffles and Roquefort cheese.

Meanwhile, the giant US-based shipping company, United Parcel Service (UPS), has been lobbying Washington to take Canada's government-run postal service to the WTO dispute panel. UPS says that Ottawa is unfairly subsidizing Canada Post and therefore poaching potential customers. Ottawa in its turn has announced its intention to prohibit the export of fresh water from Canada by a California-based company.

And so it goes in the topsy-turvy new world of economic globalization. Those institutions which first emerged from the Bretton Woods negotiations half a century ago have become more important players with each passing decade. It is their vision and their agenda which continue to shape the direction of the global economy. Together, they are fostering a model of liberalized trade and investment which is heartily endorsed by the world's biggest banks and corporations. A deregulated, privatized, corporate-led free market is the answer to humanity's problems, they tell us. The proof, though, is not so easily found.

1 'WTO must correct imbalances against South', Martin Khor, Third World Network Features, October 1999.

3 Debt and structural adjustment

Developing countries fight for a New International Economic Order including fairer terms of trade and push their case through UN agencies like UNCTAD and producer cartels like OPEC. Petrodollars flood Northern financial centers and President Nixon floats the dollar, sabotaging the Bretton Woods fixed exchange-rate system. When Third World debt expands the IMF and World Bank step in to bail out debt-strapped nations. In return they must adopt 'structural adjustment' policies which favor cheap exports and spread poverty throughout the South.

THE WORLD HAS changed so dramatically in the last half century that it's hard to believe that only four decades ago the newly emerging colonies of Africa and Asia were joining with their nominally independent brethren in Latin America to push for a 'new international economic order' (NIEO). Throughout the 1960s and early 1970s an insistent demand for radical change burst forth from the two-thirds of the world's people who lived outside the privileged circle of North America and Western Europe. There was a powerful movement to shake off the legacy of colonialism and to fight for a new global system based on economic justice between nations.

Some Third World nations began to explore ways of increasing their bargaining power with the industrialized countries in Europe and North America by taking advantage of their control over key resources. Groups like the Organization of Petroleum Exporting Countries (OPEC) hoped to cooperate together to control the supply of petroleum and ratchet up the price of oil, thereby increasing their share of global wealth and bringing prosperity to their populations. There was heady talk of 'producer cartels' to raise the price of exports like sugar, coffee, cocoa, tin and rubber. That way poor countries that were critically dependent on one or two primary commodities could gain more income and more control over their own development. There was also strong and vocal opposition to the growing power of transnational corporations who were seen to be remaking the world in their own interests. But when poor countries did try to force up the price of their primary exports they often found themselves faced with near-monopoly control by Western corporations of processing, distribution and marketing. When the declaration of principles for an NIEO was issued in 1974 it was the culmination of a new 'solidarity of the oppressed' which had spread throughout the developing nations.

Galvanized by centuries-old colonial injustices and sparked by the radical ideas of Fanon in Algeria, Nkrumah in Ghana, Gandhi in India, Sukarno in Indonesia, Nyerere in Tanzania and Castro in Latin America, these 'Third World' nations set out to collectively challenge the entrenched power of the United States and Western Europe. The NIEO was not a grass-roots movement. It was a collection of progressive intellectuals and politicians who believed correctly that, left on their own, free markets would never reduce global inequalities. Instead these leaders argued for improved 'terms of trade' and a more just international economic system. When bargaining failed producer countries began to form trade alliances based on specific commodities.

Third World nations came together in political organizations like the Non-Aligned Movement which was initially an attempt to break out of the polarized East/West power struggle between the West and the Soviet Bloc. In the United Nations, developing countries formed the 'Group of 77' which was instrumental in creating the UN Conference on Trade and Development (UNCTAD). Within UNCTAD poor countries pushed for fairer 'terms of trade'. Many newly-independent countries of the South still relied heavily on the export of raw materials in the 1950s and 1960s. But there was a faltering effort and a stronger belief in the need to build local industrial capacities and to support the push for a 'new international economic order'. Why was it, they asked, that the price of everything they imported from the West, whether it was manufactured goods, spare parts or foodstuffs, seemed to creep ever upwards while the prices they received for their agricultural exports and raw materials remained the same – or even decreased?

The transparent injustice of this enraged and frustrated leaders like Tanzania's Julius Nyerere who referred to declining terms of trade as constantly 'riding the downward escalator'. Between 1980 and 1991 alone non-oil-exporting developing countries lost nearly $290 billion due to decreasing prices for their primary commodity exports. In response to this economic discrimination Third World nations also began agitating for an increase in 'untied' aid from the West; for more liberal terms on development loans; and for a quicker transfer of new manufacturing technologies from North to South.

In addition most developing countries favored an active government role in running the national economy. They quite rightly feared that in a world of vast economic inequality they could easily be crushed between self-interested Western governments and their muscular business partners. That was the chief reason that many Third World nations began to take tentative steps to regulate foreign investment and to maintain at least minimal trade restrictions.

Latin American nations were especially successful at encouraging 'import substitution' as a way of boosting local manufacturing, employment and income. Countries like Brazil and Argentina used a mix of taxation policy, tariffs and financial incentives to attract both foreign and domestic investment. American and European auto companies set up factories to take advantage of import barriers. The development goal was to stimulate industrialization in order to produce goods locally and to boost export earnings. This had the added benefit of reducing imports, which both cut the need for scarce foreign exchange and kept domestic capital circulating inside the country. Unfortunately, the era of import substitution was short. Latin American nations were soon bullied into dismantling import barriers so that by the late 1960s there were no local producers of cars, TVs, ice-boxes/fridges or other major household goods. Still, this was a brief but important step in trying to shift the balance of global power to poor countries.

New economic order

But even before the clamor for a new world economic order, momentous changes were beginning to unfold that would dramatically alter the fate of poor nations for decades to come. By the late 1960s the Bretton Woods dream of a stable monetary system of fixed exchange rates with the dollar as the only international currency was collapsing under the strain of American trade and budgetary deficits.

The United States' economy was firing on all cylinders and beginning to dangerously overheat. As the war in Vietnam escalated, the Federal Reserve in Washington pumped out millions of dollars to finance the conflict. Inflation edged upwards and the US foreign debt ballooned to pay for the war.

World Bank President Robert McNamara also leapt into the fray and contracted huge loans to the South during the 1970s – both for 'development' (essentially defined as basic infrastructure to bring 'backward' economies into the market system) and to act as a bulwark against a perceived worldwide communist threat. The Bank's stake in the South increased five-fold over the decade.

At the same time a guarded optimism took hold in the South, fueled by moderately-high growth rates and a short-term boom in the price of primary commodities, particularly oil. The Organization of Petroleum Exporting Countries (OPEC) was the first, and ultimately the most successful, Third World 'producer union'. By standing together and controlling the supply of oil they were able to increase the price of petroleum three-fold to over $30 a barrel. The result was windfall surpluses for OPEC members – $310 billion for the period 1972-1977 alone. This 'oil shock' rippled through the global economy, triggering double-digit inflation and a massive 'recycling' problem.

What were OPEC nations to do with this vast new wealth of 'petrodollars'? Some of it they would spend on glittering new airports, power stations and other showcase mega-projects. But much of it eventually wound up as investment in Northern financial centers or deposited in Northern commercial banks. This was the birth of the 'eurocurrency' market – a huge pool of cash held outside the borders of the countries that originally issued the currency. The US dollar was the main 'eurocurrency' but there were also francs, guilders, marks and pounds.

Western banks, flush with this new OPEC money, then began to search for borrowers. They didn't have long to look. Soon millions in loans were contracted to non-oil-producing Third World governments desperate to pay escalating fuel bills and to fund ambitious development goals. At the same time the massive increase in oil prices helped inflation soar around the world. Prices skyrocketed while growth slowed to a crawl and a new word was added to the lexicon of economists: 'stagflation'. In the midst of this economic chaos US President Richard Nixon moved unilaterally to de-link the dollar from gold. As a result the world moved to a system of floating exchange rates. Nixon also devalued the greenback (US dollar) against other major world currencies and jacked up interest rates, a move which had an enormous impact on the global economy.

By slashing the value of the dollar Washington effectively reduced the huge debt it owed to the rest of the world. The US had been running a large deficit in order to pay the costs of the war in Vietnam. As interest rates shot up, those countries reeling under OPEC oil-price hikes had the cost of their eurodollar loans (most of which were denominated in US dollars) double and even triple, almost overnight. The debt of the non-oil producing Third World increased five-fold between 1973 and 1982, reaching a staggering $612 billion. The banks were desperate to lend to meet their interest obligations on deposits so easy terms were the order of the day. Dictators who could exact payments from their cowering populations with relative ease must have seemed like a good bet for lenders looking for a secure return.

Sometimes the petrodollar loan money was squandered on grandiose and ill-considered projects. Sometimes it was simply filched – siphoned off by Third World élites into personal accounts in the same Northern banks that had made the original loans. Often it was both wasted and stolen.

Foolish loans

The experience was similar across the South. From the mid-1960s to the mid-1980s, despotism pervaded Latin America and employed an ingenious variety of scams wherever it went. In Asia and Africa, megalomaniacs with powerful friends and large appetites for personal wealth were financed with enthusiasm by the international banking fraternity. Indeed, it seemed to work so well that the credit lines became almost limitless – particularly if the governments in question were fighting on the right side of the Cold War and buying large quantities of armaments from Northern suppliers.

Examples of these foolish loans to corrupt leaders are well known. In the Philippines, dictator Ferdinand Marcos along with his wife Imelda and their cronies are estimated to have pocketed in the form of kick-

Debt and structural adjustment

Africa's hidden killers

People are dying quietly, but in huge numbers, all over Zambia. Not because of some accident of nature but as a direct result of economic policies imposed by faceless Western planners. For over 20 years the World Bank and the International Monetary Fund have been forcing structural adjustment programs (SAPs) on the bankrupt countries of Africa, blind to the havoc they are causing. Almost every country on the continent has succumbed.

'If you want to see the impact of structural adjustment,' says Emily Sikazwe, director of the antipoverty group Women for Change, 'go to University Teaching Hospital (UTH) in Lusaka.'

In a packed ward in UTH, the city's biggest hospital, emaciated figures shiver under sparse bedclothes. Families crowd around, bringing food to the sick to supplement the meager hospital rations of beans and maize meal. In another ward rows of children lie on small beds, slowly passing away from preventable diseases like TB, malaria and pneumonia.

In a cleaner, neater ward on the other side of the building half the beds stand empty. This is the fee-paying section where families who can pay a 100,000 kwacha ($40) deposit can buy a slightly better chance of life. This is what some World Bank bureaucrats refer to as 'user-responsive' healthcare.

Meanwhile in the shantytown of Misisi four out of five people are unemployed, part of an army of jobless created when economists from the World Bank and IMF decided that Zambia's public sector was 'bloated' and would benefit from the tonic of privatization. But half the state-owned companies sold are now bankrupt and thousands are out of work. Others like Esnart Banda, a widow with five children, survive against the odds. She makes about 2,000 kwacha ($0.60) a day selling vegetables in a market near Misisi. Most days she can only afford one meal for her children, even though the youngest is suffering from TB. Her kids join the 40 per cent of Zambia's child population suffering from chronic undernutrition.

'Africa can only develop with the participation of its people,' says Emily Sikazwe.' This is what Zambian NGOs are now focusing on. They are demanding that Africans be allowed to decide how their countries are run. But if IMF and World Bank economists are to respect this demand they will have to leave their plush offices in Washington to visit Lusaka and, if they're serious, UTH and Misisi. And for once they'll need to listen to what people there say. ■

Mark Lynas is a freelance writer specializing in environment and development issues.

backs and commissions a third of all loans to that country. Before he was forced out of office, Marcos' personal wealth was estimated at $10 billion.

Meanwhile, there are no records for 80 per cent of the $40 billion borrowed by the Argentinean military dictatorship from 1976 to 1983. Argentineans are demanding that their Government either produce accounts or have the debts declared illegal. It seems that New York banks knew money was being misused, that there had been kickbacks and fraudulent loans to companies linked to the military, and that the IMF allegedly connived with the fraud. It is also clear that the military used some of the loans to buy weapons for the Falklands/Malvinas War.

Deeper in debt

From 1997 to the first year of the millennium, the 'Jubilee 2000' citizens' movement led a worldwide campaign to cancel the debts of the world's poorest countries. Jubilee researchers found that almost a quarter of all Third World debt (nearly $500 billion) is the result of loans used to prop up dictators in some 25 different countries. [1]

The money flowed free and fast through the 1980s and early 1990s. But eventually the soaring tower of debt began to creak and sway. One government after the next began to run into financial trouble. The loans they had raised and squandered on daft projects or salted away in private bank accounts became so large their foreign exchange earnings and tax revenues couldn't keep up the payments.

During this period the IMF became an enforcer of tough policy conditions on poor countries that were forced to apply to the Fund for temporary balance-of-payments assistance. During the 1970s and early 1980s the IMF's loans were conditional on governments following the advice of the Fund's economists who had their own take on what Southern nations were doing wrong and how they could fix it. The Fund's demands were woven into the deals worked out with those countries that required an immediate transfusion of cash. Essentially, the agency argued that the debtor country's problems were caused by 'excessive demand' in the domestic economy. Curiously, the responsibility of the private banks who made most of the dubious loans in the first place (with their eyes wide open it should be noted) was ignored.

The IMF prescription

According to the Fund this excessive demand meant there were too many imports and not enough exports. The solution was to devalue the currency and cut government spending. This was supposed to slow the economy and reduce domestic demand, gradually resulting in fewer imports, along with more, and cheaper, exports. In time, the IMF argued, the balance-of-payments deficit would be eliminated. Countries were more or less forced to adopt these austerity measures if they wanted to get the IMF 'seal of approval'. Without it they would be ostracized on the fringes of the global economy. Both the IMF and the World Bank also urged debtor nations to take on deeper 'structural adjustment' measures as early as the 1970s but borrowing countries refused to go along with the advice.

Then in 1982 Mexico told its creditors it could no longer pay and a full-fledged Third World 'debt crisis' emerged. Northern politicians and bankers began to worry that the sheer volume of unpayable loans would undermine the world financial system. Widespread panic began to sweep through the world of international finance as scores of Southern nations teetered on the brink of economic collapse. In response both the Bank and the IMF hardened their line and began to demand major changes in the way debtor nations ran their domestic economies. Countries like Ghana were forced to toe the line and enforce tough adjustment conditions as early as 1983.

A few years later, the US Treasury Secretary James Baker decided to formalize this new strategy to force Third World economies to radically 'restructure' their economies to meet their debt obligations. The 'Baker Plan' was introduced at the 1985 meeting of the World Bank and the IMF when both agencies were called on to impose more thorough 'adjustments' to the economic policies of debtor countries.

The Bank and the Fund made full use of this new leverage. Together they launched a policy to 'structurally adjust' the Third World by deflating economies and demanding a withdrawal of government – not only from public enterprise but also from compassionate support of the basic health and welfare of the most vulnerable. Exports to earn foreign exchange were privileged over basic necessities, food production and other goods for domestic use. [2]

The Fund set up its first 'formal' Structural Adjustment Facility in 1986. The World Bank soon followed, so that by 1989 the Bank had contracted adjustment loans to 75 per cent of the countries that already had similar IMF loans in place. The Bank's

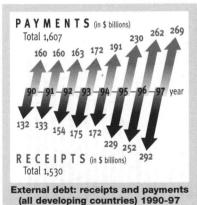

PAYMENTS (in $ billions)
Total 1,607
160 160 163 172 191 230 262 269
90 – 91 – 92 – 93 – 94 – 95 – 96 – 97 year
132 133 154 175 172 229 252 292

RECEIPTS (in $ billions)
Total 1,530

External debt: receipts and payments (all developing countries) 1990-97 ($ billions)

World Development Report 1998/9, World Bank

South pays North

Most of the increase in debt during the 1990s was to pay interest on existing loans. It was not used for productive investment or to tackle poverty. In six of the eight years from 1990 to 1997, developing countries paid out more in debt service (interest plus repayments) than they received in new loans – a total transfer from the poor South to the rich North of $77 billion. ∎

conditions both extended and reinforced the IMF prescription for financial 'liberalization' and open markets. They included 'privatizing' state-owned enterprises; reducing the size and cost of government through massive public sector layoffs; cutting basic social services and subsidies on basic foodstuffs; and reducing barriers to trade. This restructuring was highly successful from the point of view of the private banks who siphoned off more than $178 billion from the South between 1984 and 1990 alone.[3] Structural-adjustment programs (SAPs) were in fact an extremely effective mechanism for transforming private debt into public debt.

The 1980s were a 'lost decade' for much of the Third World. Growth stagnated and debt doubled to almost $1,500 billion by the decade's end. By 1999 it had reached nearly $3,000 billion. An ever-increasing

The debt mountain

The foreign debts of developing countries are more than two trillion (million million) US dollars and still growing. The result is a debt of over $400 for every man, woman and child in the developing world – where average income in the very poorest countries is less than a dollar a day. ■

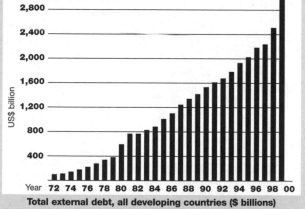

Total external debt, all developing countries ($ billions)

World Development Report 1999/00, World Bank

proportion of this new debt was to service interest payments on the old debt, to keep money circulating and to keep the system up-and-running. Most of this debt had shifted from private banks to the IMF and the World Bank – though the majority was still owed to rich countries and Northern banks. The big difference was that the Fund and the Bank were always first in line so paying them was a much more onerous prospect.

Taking more out

The stark fact that the Fund and the Bank began operating with reverse capital flows (in other words they were then taking more money out of the Third World than they were putting back in) was sobering for those who believed those institutions were there to help.

In six of the eight years from 1990 to 1997 developing countries paid out more in debt service (interest plus repayments) than they received in new loans: a total transfer from South to North of $77 billion. And most of the increase was used to meet interest payments rather than for productive investment.[4] After 1998 the balance changed again as a result of massive bailout packages to Mexico and Asia. However, this will likely set the stage for negative flows again in the near future.

The 'conditionalities' of structural adjustment meanwhile diverted government revenues away from things like education and healthcare, towards debt repayment and the promotion of exports. This gave the World Bank and IMF a degree of control that even the most despotic of colonial regimes rarely achieved.

Even former enthusiastic supporters of structural adjustment were forced to reconsider their faith in this 'neo-liberal' recipe for economic progress. In 1999, Harvard University's 'economic shock-therapy' advocate Jeffrey Sachs wrote: 'Many of the three billion of the world's poorest live in countries whose governments have long since gone bankrupt under the weight of past credits from foreign governments, banks and agencies such as the World Bank and the

IMF. These countries have become desperate wards of the IMF... Their debts should be canceled outright and the IMF sent home.' [5]

The situation has remained essentially unchanged ever since. In nations as far apart as Yugoslavia, Rwanda and Peru, the privations suffered in the name of debt repayments lay concealed behind outbreaks of violent civil unrest. All attempts to organize relief for the South were rebuffed on principle until 1996, when the 'Heavily Indebted Poor Countries Initiative' was launched to make debt repayments 'sustainable'. Within a decade, the 'cold' war which ended in 1989 was replaced by a 'financial' war that is still being fought.

Two decades of structural adjustment has not only failed to solve the debt crisis, it has caused untold suffering for millions and led to widening gaps between rich and poor. A 1999 study by the Washington-based group, Development Gap, looked at the impact of SAPs

Creating poverty

In return for new loans to poor countries, lenders in the 1980s and 1990s insisted on 'structural adjustment' to increase their chances of being paid back. This meant cutting government spending on things like healthcare and education – the very services on which poor people (and women and children in particular) rely. Many of these countries have ended up spending more on servicing their debts than on the basic needs of their citizens. ■

Debt interest payments as % government revenue*		Social services as % government expenditure**
75.6	Brazil	34.5
41.2	Bulgaria	35.0
23.0	Cameroon	29.0
57.8	Guatemala	38.4
33.6	India	11.9
31.7	Kenya	27.1
59.9	Madagascar	34.6

* Expenditure frequently exceeds revenue, so totals may exceed 100%
** Includes health, education, social security, welfare, housing and community services

Government spending on foreign debt and social services (selected countries, 1995)

World Development Report 1998/9, World Bank

on more than 70 African and Asian countries during the early 1990s. The study concluded that the longer a country operates under structural adjustment the worse its debt burden becomes. SAPs, Development Gap warned, 'are likely to push countries into a tragic circle of debt, adjustment, a weakened domestic economy, heightened vulnerability and greater debt.' [6]

Debt's legacy

So we are left with a bizarre and degrading spectacle. In Africa, external debt has ballooned by 400 per cent since the Bank and the IMF began managing national economies through structural adjustment. Today in Ethiopia a hundred thousand children die annually from easily preventable diseases, while debt repayments are four times more than public spending on healthcare. In Tanzania, where 40 per cent of people die before the age of 35, debt payments are 6 times greater than spending on healthcare. From the whole of Africa, where one in every two children of primary-school age is not in school, governments transfer four times more to Northern creditors in debt payments than they spend on the health and education of their citizens.

Structural-adjustment programs may not have put Third World countries back on a steady economic keel but they have certainly helped undermine democracy in those nations. Joseph Stiglitz, former World Bank Chief Economist, is candid about the record of bureaucrats in both agencies undermining the ability of nominally independent nation states to govern their own affairs. In an article written shortly after his resignation Stiglitz said there are 'real risks associated with delegating excessive power to international agencies... The institution can actually become an interest group itself, concerned with maintaining its position and advancing its power.' If we believe in democratic processes he continues, 'countries must make the decisions for themselves, and the responsibility of economic advisors is only to appraise them of prevailing views.' [2]

Debt and structural adjustment

The debt load on all governments, but particularly those of the Third World, has crippled their capacity to look after their citizens. Capital moves so freely that it is often impossible for governments to find, let alone tax.

With the disintegration of the Soviet Union, the impoverishment of Africa and the resurgence of an unfettered market system in Asia and Latin America the triumph of capitalism seems complete. Indeed, SAPs really only make sense when seen through the lens of economic globalization. They are an integral part of the free-market orthodoxy which aims to give free rein to private corporations to trade, invest and move capital around the globe with a minimum amount of government interference.

But there are cracks emerging in this seemingly uniform consensus. People in the South are resisting structural adjustment through violent opposition and grassroots organizing. Protest too is coming from the millions uprooted by World Bank mega-projects, particularly the building of massive hydroelectric dams. Rejection of all things Western is on the rise. Fundamentalism and the politics of ethnic exclusion (from Somalia to Kosovo to India) are turning political costs into military ones. And, as the Seattle protests of December 1999 illustrated, powerful and unaccountable institutions like the World Trade Organization are coming under direct pressure from citizens' groups, community activists, students, trade unionists and environmentalists. Many are calling for reform. Others are going much farther and demanding the outright abolition of these agencies and a complete restructuring of the global financial architecture.

1 'Take the hit!' by Joseph Hanlon, *New Internationalist*, No 312, May 1999; **2** *Economic Justice Report*, Ecumenical Coalition for Economic Justice, Vol X, No 4, December 1999; **3** 'How Bretton Woods re-ordered the world', *New Internationalist*, No 257, July 1994; **4** 'Debt: the facts', *New Internationalist*, No 312, May 1999; **5** *The Independent*, London, Feb 1, 1999; **6** 'Conditioning debt relief on adjustment: creating conditions for more indebtedness', Development Gap, Washington 1999.

4 The corporate century

Giant private companies have become the driving force behind economic globalization, wielding more power than many nation-states. Business values of efficiency and competition at all costs now dominate the debate on social policy, the public interest and the role of government. The tendency to monopoly combined with decreasing rates of profit drives and structures corporate decision-making – without regard for the social, environmental and economic consequences of those decisions.

WHETHER YOU WALK the streets of New York or Nairobi, Beijing or Buenos Aires, globalization has introduced a level of commercial culture which is eerily homogenous. The glittering, air-conditioned shopping malls are interchangeable; the fast food restaurants sell the same high carbohydrate foods with minor concessions to local tastes. Young people drink the same soft drinks, smoke the same cigarettes, wear identical branded clothing and shoes, play the same computer games, watch the same Hollywood films and listen to the same Western pop music.

Welcome to the world of the multinational corporation, a cultural and economic *tsunami* (tidal wave) that is roaring across the globe and replacing the spectacular diversity of human society with a Westernized version of the good life. As corporations market the consumer dream of wealth and glamor, local cultures around the world are eroded. Family and community bonds are disintegrating as social relationships are 'commodified' and reduced to what Karl Marx called the 'crude cash nexus'. In the words of sociologist Helena Norberg-Hodge, there is 'a global monoculture which is now able to disrupt traditional cultures with a shocking speed and finality and which surpasses anything the world has witnessed before.' [1]

Over the past two decades, as the global rules regulating the movement of goods and investment have been relaxed, private corporations have expanded their global reach so that their decisions now touch the lives of people in the most distant parts of the world. The vast, earth-straddling companies dominate global trade in everything from computers and pharmaceuticals to insurance, banking and cinema. Their holdings are so numerous and so Byzantine that it is often impossible to trace the chain of ownership. Even so it is estimated that a third of all trade in the $4 trillion international economy is actually business between branches of the same corporation.

Some proponents of globalization argue that multinationals are the ambassadors of democracy. They insist that free markets and political freedoms are inextricably bound together and that the introduction of the first will inevitably lead to the second. Unfortunately, the facts don't support their claim. Market economies flourish in some of the world's most autocratic and tyrannical states and multinational corporations have shown surprisingly little interest in, and have had even less effect on, changing political systems. Singapore, Malaysia, Indonesia, Pakistan, Russia, Colombia: all have thriving market systems where multinational corporations are dominant actors. But they can be scarcely be counted among the world's healthy democracies.

As the American political scientist Benjamin Barber has written: 'Capitalism requires consumers with access to markets and a stable political climate in order to succeed; such conditions may or may not be fostered by democracy, which can be disorderly and even anarchic in its early stages, and which often pursues public goods costly to or at odds with private market imperatives.' Barber concludes: 'Capitalists may be democrats but capitalism does not need or entail democracy.'[2]

The UN Development Program (UNDP) notes in its 1999 *Human Development Report* that many global corporations now wield more economic power than nation-states. Today 50 of the largest 100 economies in the world are run by multinationals, not by countries. Mitsubishi is bigger than Saudi Arabia; General Motors is larger than either Greece, Norway or South Africa. The combined annual revenues of the biggest 200 corporations are greater than those of 182 nation-states that contain 80 per cent of the world's population. [3]

Of course large companies have not just appeared on the scene. They've been with us since the early days of European expansion overseas when governments routinely granted economic 'adventurers' like the Hudson Bay Company and the East India Company the right to control vast swaths of the planet in an attempt to consolidate imperial rule. But there has been nothing in history to match the economic mus-

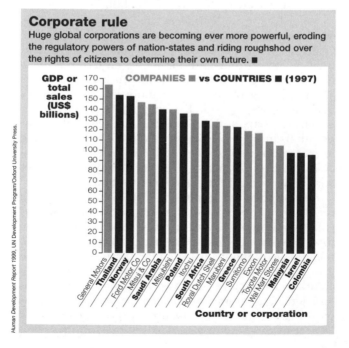

Corporate rule

Huge global corporations are becoming ever more powerful, eroding the regulatory powers of nation-states and riding roughshod over the rights of citizens to determine their own future. ■

Human Development Report 1999, UN Development Program/Oxford University Press.

cle and political clout of today's giants. And they grow larger and more powerful by the day. Scarcely a week goes by without another union between major corporations. The global competition for market share over the past decade has been the catalyst for the biggest shift towards monopoly in the last century.

In January 2000 the world's biggest Internet provider America Online (AOL) announced a proposed $160-billion merger with Time-Warner. Then the UK-based music giant EMI also unveiled plans for a $20 billion liaison with Time-Warner – creating the world's largest music firm. Other recent mergers include the purchase of Chrysler Motors by the German firm Daimler-Benz for $43 billion; the takeover of Sprint Corporation by MCI WorldCom for $115 billion; and the purchase of the pharmaceutical giant Ciba-Geigy by Sandoz for $36 billion.

According to UN figures the tendency towards monopoly is growing across a range of industries. Concentration is taking place especially in banking and finance, media and entertainment, and communication technologies. But high-profile business marriages are also taking place in older industries like automobiles and transport as well as in primary resources like mining, forestry and agriculture. The ten largest corporations in their field now control 86 per cent of the telecommunications sector, 85 per cent of the pesticides industry, 70 per cent of the computer industry and 35 per cent of the pharmaceutical industry.

According to the accounting firm KPMG, 1999 was a record year for global mergers and acquisitions (M&As) with the total value hitting $608 billion in the first nine months alone. Stock markets reward the merged corporations with higher share prices on the grounds that the new larger firms will be more 'efficient' and therefore increase company earnings. But 'efficient' for whom? Mergers squander vast amounts of resources for no productive purpose. The public impact of this very private decision-making process is rarely considered. When two corporate giants merge it inevitably leads to thousands of job losses and scores of factory closings. In fact this is precisely the point of corporate cannibalism, to bolster the bottom line by trimming costs. For example when the UK firms Glaxo and Wellcome merged in early 1999 a tenth of the total workforce (7,500 workers) lost their jobs. Good news for shareholders, but not so good news if you were one of the workers who received your dismissal notice.

Merging businesses

Business executives champion the economic 'common sense' of mergers and push for their approval on the grounds that getting bigger is the only way to compete in a lean-and-mean global marketplace. But while size does matter in terms of a company's ability to compete, ironically a smaller number of large companies also heightens the tendency towards monopoly by eliminating competition. The easiest way to get rid of a competitor is to buy them out. Giant companies also have greater powers to wrest concessions from national and regional governments simply because they are such dominant economic players, creating jobs (albeit fewer of them) and boosting national income.

The spate of mergers and acquisitions over the last few years reflects the quickly changing nature of the global economy, especially the relaxation of regulations around foreign investment and the liberalization of international capital flows. Companies are now free to compete globally, to grow and expand into overseas markets – and the new international climate of free trade in goods, services and investment capital is furthering this consolidation.

The assumption that competition is good 'in and of itself' is central to the current dominant neo-liberal economic model. It's this credo that has led to a worldwide campaign in favor of privatization of publicly-owned enterprises. According to this view, government must be downsized and its role in the provision of public services curtailed. The neo-liberals argue that governments are inefficient, bloated bureaucracies that waste taxpayers' money – so they must be hobbled and restrained. There was just enough truth in this analysis for critics of big government to win new converts and gain international credibility in the late 1970s. But rather than strengthen the role of the State by streamlining bureaucratic inefficiencies, they argued that private business should do the job instead.

This manic enthusiasm for privatization exploded when Margaret Thatcher came to power in Britain in 1979. State-owned enterprises were quickly sold off: the national airline, government-run water, gas, telephone and electric utilities, and the railway system. From 1979 to 1994 the overall number of jobs in the

Engulf and Devour, Inc.

Globalization has sparked a frenzy of corporate mergers and acquisitions (M&As). These new mega-corporations threaten competition and increase the risk of monopoly.

In 1997 more than $1.6 trillion was spent on corporate M&As – 58 of these deals were worth more than $1 billion each. Most M&As have been in financial services, telecommunications, insurance, life sciences and the media. ■

Big deals

Buyer	Acquisition	Value ($US billion)
Vodafone Airtouch	Mannesmann	$183
Exxon	Mobil	$80
Glaxo Wellcome	SmithKline Beecham	$76

Cross-border mergers and acquisitions (1992-97)

The annual number of M&As doubled between 1990 and 1997 when the total value reached $236 billion.

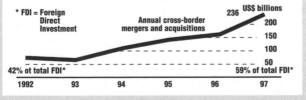

* FDI = Foreign Direct Investment

Annual cross-border mergers and acquisitions

236 US$ billions

200
150
100
50

42% of total FDI*   59% of total FDI*

1992   93   94   95   96   97

Human Development Report 1999, UN Development Program / Oxford University Press.

public sector in the UK was reduced from seven million to five million. During the same period the number of new jobs created by the private sector was minimal and the bulk of those jobs were in the non-unionized, low-paid, service sector. For a one-off payment to the public purse the British Government sold state-owned enterprises that had contributed guaranteed, yearly profits to the Treasury.

While much was made of the opportunity for ordinary British people to buy shares in the newly-privatized public utilities, the reality was quite different. Nine million UK residents did buy shares but most of them invested less than £1,000 and sold them quickly when they found they could turn a quick profit. The majority of shares of the former publicly-owned companies are now controlled by institutional investors and wealthy individuals. Author Susan George has called privatization 'one of the greatest hold-ups of our or any generation'. Nothing more, she says, than 'the alienation and surrender of the product of decades of work by thousands of people to a tiny minority of large investors.' [4]

In addition, as governments adopt the private enterprise model and cut back public expenditure they open up areas to market forces that were previously considered the responsibility of the State. After World War Two politicians in the West were forced by a civic-minded electorate to expand social welfare policies including education, healthcare, unemployment insurance, state pensions and other social security measures. At the same time the State expanded its role in the provision of public infrastructure, building roads, bridges, dams, airports, prisons and hospitals.

Now, with the notion of the 'inefficient' public sector firmly fixed in peoples' minds, governments are selling off public utilities like water, electricity and airports. Even prisons and parks are being privatized as governments pare public expenditure to meet market demands for balanced budgets. Make no mistake about it, these areas offer tremendous scope for profits. In the US alone the total budget for prisons and jails in 1997 was more than $31 billion.

Other areas are also being eyed enthusiastically by the profit-making sector. State-funded healthcare is a case in point. In Canada, Britain, Australia and Europe private companies are making major inroads into publicly-financed healthcare as deficit-conscious politicians slash budgets. At the international level, the General Agreement on Trade in Services (GATS) which is administered by the World Trade Organization (WTO) was created in 1994. One of the goals of the GATS is to classify the public health sector as part of the 'service industry', eventually opening the door to full-scale commercialization along the lines of the American model where private corporations are dominant.

The for-profit health sector in the US has been actively lobbying to pave the way for their overseas expansion. A document by the US Coalition of Service Industries in November 1999 suggested that Washington push the WTO to 'encourage more privatization' and to provide 'market access and national treatment allowing provision of all healthcare services cross-border'. The ultimate goal was clearly spelled out: to allow 'majority foreign ownership of healthcare facilities'. The dry, technical language of the market is already infecting the debate around healthcare policy. But the great fear for those defending universal, state-funded healthcare is that privatization will lead to a two-tier system where wealthy patients pay for quick, high-tech care while the rest of us put up with poorly equipped, under-funded hospitals, long waiting lists and overworked doctors, nurses and technicians.

Privatization has been strongly endorsed by both the World Bank and the IMF and is a standard ingredient in any 'structural adjustment' prescription. It is based on the notion that governments really have no business in the marketplace and that the least government is the best government. Countries are forced both to privatize public assets and to court foreign investment in their own private sector. But investment by foreign corporations is by no means a guarantee of economic progress.

For example a large part of foreign direct investment (FDI) is made up of companies' buying out state firms, purchasing equity in local companies or financing mergers and acquisitions. Cross-border M&As accounted for 59 per cent of total foreign direct investment in 1977. None of this really ends up in new productive activity and there may even be a net loss of jobs as a result of downsizing after mergers are completed. Increased investment from abroad can also result in a net drain on foreign exchange as multinational companies remit profits to their overseas headquarters. If a foreign corporation produces mainly for local markets, and especially if it edges out local suppliers rather than replacing imports, then it may significantly worsen balance of payments problems.

Controlling foreign investment

In other words it's not the quantity of FDI that matters but the quality. National governments need to select the kinds of foreign investment that will produce net benefits for their citizens and reject those investments whose overall impact will be negative. Foreign investment can make a positive contribution to national development but only if it is channeled into productive rather than speculative activities. At the moment that power to influence the quality of investment is dwindling as free-trade arrangements and bilateral trade agreements effectively tie the hands of states which agree to them, inevitably compromising government sovereignty.

Nonetheless, most Southern governments are keen on attracting investment from multinationals – despite the concern about corporate power and unethical behavior. Multinationals are extremely skilled at delivering the goods. They are at the cutting edge of technological innovation and they can introduce new management and marketing strategies. It's also true that wages and working conditions are usually better in foreign subsidiaries of multinational firms than in local companies.

But foreign investors don't automatically favor countries simply because they've loosened regulations as a result of structural adjustment. In fact the big money predictably goes to where it's safest and where the potential for quick profits is greatest. According to data from UNDP's 1999 *Human Development Report* most direct investment is concentrated in a small number of developing countries. In 1997 almost 70 per cent of all FDI to the South and the ex-Soviet bloc went to just ten countries and the bulk of that went to just one country – China.

Draining the public purse

On the other hand, in the same year nearly 60 per cent of all foreign investment went to industrial countries. Yet even in countries of the Organization for Economic Cooperation and Development (OECD) corporations have the upper hand, trading off one nation against another to see who can offer the most lucrative investment incentives. Governments drain the public purse in their attempts to buy jobs from private investors. Tax holidays, interest-free loans, grants, training schemes, unhindered profit remittances and publicly-funded sewers, roads and utilities are among the mix of 'incentives' that companies now expect in return for opening up a new factory or office.

The largest multinationals call themselves 'global firms' which might lead one to believe that they are stateless, disembodied entities toiling for the good of humankind. The truth is more complex. There are few giant companies that are truly stateless; most are firmly tied to one national home base. Microsoft and Disney are identifiably US corporations, Nortel Networks is Canadian, Bertelsmann is German, RTZ is

British and Broken Hill Pty is Australian. These companies have no problem wrapping themselves in the national flag when it comes to hitting up local governments for tax breaks, start-up grants or other goodies. But at the same time their allegiances are fickle – and quickly diverted if opportunities for profit appear greater elsewhere. The fact that multinational corporations are relatively footloose means they can move operations to where costs are cheapest – and play off one government against another in the process. This political power – to pull up stakes, lay off workers and shift production elsewhere – is a powerful bargaining chip which business can use to wrest greater concessions from job-hungry governments.

One of the corporate sector's greatest political victories in recent decades has been to beat down corporate taxes. In Britain, the corporate tax rate fell from 52 per cent in 1979 to 30 per cent in 2000 and Labor Prime Minister Tony Blair has boasted that British business is subject to even fewer strictures than corporations in the US. Corporate tax rates have declined in virtually every OECD country over the last two decades as governments rely more and more on personal income taxes and sales taxes for revenues. In 1950 corporate taxes in the US accounted for 30 per cent of government funds; today they account for less than 12 per cent.

Their sheer size, wealth and power means that multinationals and the business sector in general have been able to structure the public debate on social issues and the role of government in a way which benefits their own interests. They have used their louder voices and political clout to build an effective propaganda machine and to boost what the great Italian political theorist Antonio Gramsci called their 'cultural hegemony'. Through sophisticated public relations, media manipulation and friends-in-high-places the neo-liberal economic perspective has come to be accepted as the 'common sense' approach to running a country. This radical paradigm shift has occurred in the short space of 30 years.

A corporation's ultimate responsibility is to its shareholders, as Chief Executive Officers (CEOs) constantly reassure their investors at annual general meetings. It is enhanced value for shareholders which drives and structures corporate decision-making – without regard for the social, environmental and economic consequences of those decisions. Unless obligations to the public good are imposed on companies the business agenda will continue to ride roughshod over national and community interests.

The North American Free Trade Agreement (NAFTA) was one of the first regional economic pacts developed to further corporate globalization. The Washington-based, non-governmental organization, Public Citizen, has documented a steady movement of American companies to cheap labor zones in Mexico and the direct loss of hundreds of thousands of jobs since NAFTA came into effect in 1995.

The activist group cites the example of the jeans maker Guess? Inc. which, according to the *Wall Street Journal*, cut the percentage of its clothes sewn in Los Angeles from 97 per cent prior to NAFTA to 35 per cent two years later. In that period the company relocated five sewing factories to Mexico and others to Peru and Chile. More than 1,000 Guess? workers in Los Angeles lost their jobs. At the same time the Public Citizen group notes that corporate supporters of the trade deal can't provide documentation for more than a few thousand NAFTA job gains.

And while most jobs lost to NAFTA were in high-paying manufacturing, the ones that replaced them were in the low-paid, non-unionized service sector. NAFTA also had a negative effect on the wages of US workers whose jobs have not been relocated. They are now in direct competition with skilled, educated Mexican workers who work for a dollar or two an hour – or less. As a result their bargaining power with their employers has been substantially lessened. NAFTA was supposed to solve this problem by raising Mexican living standards and wages. Instead, both have plummeted, harming the economic prospects for workers on both sides of the border.

The upper hand

As corporations gain the upper hand, the fear of job losses and the resulting social devastation has created a downward pressure on environmental standards and social programs – what critics of unregulated corporate power call 'a race to the bottom'.

Treaties like NAFTA, and new trade rules backed by the WTO, empower corporations while restricting national governments from interfering with the 'wisdom' of the market. But business is constantly pushing to expand the freedom to trade and invest, unhindered by either government regulations or social obligations. The Multilateral Agreement on Investment (MAI), described below, is the most infamous recent example of the attempt by big business to remake the world in its image.

Public disillusionment with the WTO is now well known and opposition is growing to the organization's bottom-line brand of globalization. But if activists hadn't stumbled across the MAI in 1997, efforts to inject human values into the debate on the global trading system could have been severely curtailed. After the WTO came into being in 1994, the globe's major corporations began to put together a plan for codifying the rules of world trade in a way that would give them complete freedom. They found it in the MAI, an agreement which was drafted by the International Chamber of Commerce (a 'professional association' of the world's largest companies) and presented to the rich-nation OECD members for discussion and, it was assumed, rubber-stamp approval.[5]

Once passed, the next stop was to be the WTO. Third World governments were rightly suspicious of the MAI

and many saw it as 'a throwback to colonial era economics'. But, with the weight of the OECD behind it,
supporters of the MAI reckoned it would be speedily
adopted as an official WTO document.

Delegates from OECD countries began discussing
the MAI in early 1995 behind closed doors. By early
1997 most of the treaty was down on paper and the
public was none the wiser. In fact, most politicians in
the OECD's 29 member countries weren't even aware
of the negotiations. It was only when activists in
Canada got their hands on a copy of the MAI and
began sending it around the world via the Internet
that the full scope of the document became clear.

The MAI was a corporate dream come true.
Essentially the agreement set out to give private companies the same legal status as nation-states in all
countries that were party to the Agreement. But more
importantly it set out a clear set of rules so that corporations would be able to defend their new rights
against the objections of sovereign governments. The
MAI was so overwhelmingly biased towards the interests of multinationals that critics were quick to label it
'the corporate rule treaty'.

For example, under MAI provisions corporations
could sue governments for passing laws that might
reduce their potential profits. They could make their
case in secret with no outside interest groups involved
and the decision would be binding. The MAI also
allowed foreign investors to challenge public funding
of social programs as a distortion of free markets and
the 'level playing field'. If a government chose to privatize a state-owned industry it could no longer give
preference to domestic buyers. In addition, governments would be forbidden to demand that foreign
investment benefit local communities or the national
economy. They could not demand domestic content,
local hiring, affirmative action, technology transfer or
anything else in return for allowing foreign companies
to exploit publicly owned resources. And there were to

be no limits on profit repatriation.

Once the text became public, citizens' groups around the world began vigorous education campaigns on the potentially-damaging impact of the MAI. Two influential activists, Tony Clarke and Maude Barlow, summed up the feelings of citizens' groups everywhere. The MAI, they wrote, 'would provide corporations with the right to directly enforce an international treaty to which they are not party and under which they have no obligations. It would be entirely one-sided; neither citizens nor governments could sue the corporations back. The MAI would provide foreign investors with new and substantive rights with which they could challenge government programs, policies and laws all over the world.' [5]

MAI protest

In a few months public anxiety about the deal came to a head. In France, Australia, Canada and the US politicians at all levels were drawn into the debate and governments were forced to enter 'reservations' to protect themselves from certain of the MAI's provisions. By the May 1998 deadline it was clear that the talks were at a standstill and that public opposition had torpedoed further progress on the Agreement.

This was a stunning victory for a growing international citizens' movement. But the end of the MAI as such did not spell the end of the corporate agenda for an unregulated, global investment treaty. The focus would now shift to the WTO and other global venues where multinationals could lobby for the MAI-like investment provisions. As Sir Leon Brittan, vice-president of the European Commission, declared: 'Investment... seems to me the top priority of the WTO... Because it involves the development of an appropriate framework of binding rules.'

The downward pressure on wages and social programs caused by economic globalization is compounded by the rise of free trade zones (FTZs) which exist in dozens of Third World countries – there are now more than 800 FTZs operating from Malaysia and the Philippines to El Salvador, Mexico and even socialist Cuba. These officially sanctioned sites exist almost as separate countries, offering their corporate clients minimal taxes, lax environmental regulations, cheap labor and low overheads.

In their urgent effort to expand globally, corporations have ignored a fundamental aspect of capitalist production: over-capacity. It was Henry Ford, one of the pioneers of mass production, who realized 80 years ago the inherent dilemma of replacing labor with machines and then paying the remaining workers poverty-level wages. You could produce a lot of cars but in the end you would have no-one who could afford to buy them: too many goods and too few buyers. Today, a huge investment in computerized, high-tech machinery has also destroyed millions of jobs while

Korten on corporations
Critic and author **David Korten** reflects on corporate power.

Corporations say the solution to poverty is to stimulate growth and create more wealth for everyone. Do you think that approach will work?

There is little evidence that economic growth alleviates poverty. Since 1950 the world's total economic output has increased five-fold while the number of people living in absolute poverty has doubled. This growth has pushed human demands on the eco-system beyond what the planet is capable of sustaining. And that does two things: it accelerates the rate of breakdown of the planet's ability to regenerate its natural systems. And it intensifies the competition between rich and poor for the resources that remain. I now believe that what the Gross National Product (GNP) really measures is the rate at which the economically powerful are expropriating the resources of the economically weak in order to convert them into products that quickly become the garbage of the rich.

Corporate leaders and their government backers claim free trade and open markets are the only way to have an efficient market system. Does business know best?

The modern corporation is specifically designed to concentrate economic power, and to protect the people who use that power from liability for the consequences of its uses. Free-trade agreements like NAFTA and GATT are not really trade agreements at all. They are boosting productivity and constraining wage growth. Henry Ford's own automobile sector is a case in point. One of the major reasons for the massive restructuring in that industry over the past decade is over-capacity, which is estimated at more than 25 to 30 per cent worldwide. According to *The Economist* magazine the global auto industry can produce 20 million more vehicles a year than there are potential buyers.

There is a global over-capacity in everything from shoes and steel to clothing and electronic goods. One estimate puts the excess manufacturing capacity in China at more than 40 per cent. As industries consolidate to cut losses, factories are closed but output remains the same or even increases. This produces falling rates of profit which in turn drives industry to look for further efficiencies. One tack is to continue to cut labor costs – which helps the bottom line initially but actually dampens global demand over time.

economic integration agreements intended to guarantee the rights of global corporations to move both goods and investments wherever they wish – free from public interference or accountability. Corporate power really lies in this ability to manipulate communities and markets in their own interest.

As corporations replace workers with technology they gain even more clout. Local governments are now forced not only to give them tax breaks but to subsidize directly their operations as well. This is what global competition is really about – communities and workers competing against each other to absorb even more of the production costs of the world's most powerful and profitable companies.

Is sustainable growth possible?

In my view 'green growth' is an oxymoron. In a deregulated market economy global corporations are accountable to only one master, a rogue financial system with one incessant demand – keep your stock price as high as possible by maximizing short-term returns. One way to do that is to shift as much of the cost of the corporation's operations as possible onto the community. The goal is to externalize costs and privatize gain.

A green corporation simply can't last in our unregulated market economy where competing companies are not internalizing their costs. If you do attempt to 'green' your business you'll soon be bought out by some corporate raiders who see an opportunity to externalize costs and make a short-term killing. ■

Another is the merger and acquisition route – cut costs by consolidating production, closing factories and laying off workers. However, this too is self-defeating in the long run since it also inevitably reduces demand.

The real danger of this overproduction is 'deflation'. Instead of a steady rise in employment and relatively stable prices for commodities and manufactured goods, deflation results in a steady downward spiral of both prices and wages. In economic terms the logic is simple: productive capacity exceeds demand, prices fall, unemployment rises and wages are forced down even farther.

In the 1930s the result was a resounding and destructive economic crash which saw factories close and millions of workers laid off. This catastrophe was only turned around when factories boosted production of armaments and other supplies for the Second World War. So far the specter of deflation has been kept at bay by making the US economy the 'consumer of last resort'. According to the IMF, the US has provided about half the growth in total world demand since 1988. Fueled by a strong dollar and a vastly-overvalued stock market, the American economy continues to suck in cheap imports from the rest of the world. The result is colossal domestic debt and record trade deficits. In 1999 the US trade deficit soared to nearly $300 billion, almost triple the deficit of 1995.

In an era of globalized free markets all countries try and fight their way to prosperity by boosting exports. That's partly because traditional Keynesian methods of stimulating domestic growth by 'priming the pump' have fallen into disfavor and few countries now have either the inclination or the political will to direct domestic savings toward investment in the local market. Instead, all nations look outwards, depending more and more on international trade for their economic survival. This focus on trade is reflected in the data. According to the UN's Food and Agriculture Organization the value of world agricultural trade more than doubled from 1972 to 1997 – from $224 billion to $457 billion. The same was true for global trade in forest products which jumped from $47 billion in 1970 to $139 billion in 1998.

Yet, the success of any one country vis-a-vis another depends on how competitively (i.e. how cheaply) it can price its goods in the world market. This kind of competition inevitably means cutting costs and the easiest costs to cut are wages. But as we have already seen, cheap labor exports inevitably backfire by undermining domestic purchasing power and depressing domestic demand. Simply put: workers earn less so they have less to spend. As University of Ottawa economist Michel Chossudovsky notes: 'the expansion of exports from developing countries is predicated on the contraction of internal purchasing power. Poverty is an input on the supply side.' [6]

Over the past decade the UN has documented a steady shift of global income from wages to profits throughout the world. Even so investors are no longer satisfied with five or six per cent annual returns. As barriers to the free movement of capital started to crumble around the world, corporations, banks and other major investors began to cast around anxiously for other surefire means of maximizing their returns. The solution was quick at hand. From the 'real' economy of manufacturing and commodity production investors turned to the world of international finance. Speculation and gambling in international money markets seemed an easier path than competing for fewer and fewer paying customers in the old goods and services economy. The era of the 'global casino' had arrived.

1 'The march of the monoculture', Helena Norberg-Hodge, *The Ecologist*, Vol 29, No 2, May/June 1999; **2** *Jihad vs McWorld*, Benjamin R Barber, Ballantine Books, New York, 1995; **3** *Human Development Report 1999*, UN Development Program, New York/Oxford, 1999; **4** 'A short history of neoliberalism', Susan George, paper presented to the conference on Economic sovereignty in a globalizing world, Bangkok, March 1999; **5** This description of the battle against the MAI owes much to *MAI Round 2: new global and internal threats to Canadian sovereignty*, Tony Clarke and Maude Barlow, Stoddart, 1998; **6** *The globalization of poverty*, Michel Chossudovsky, Third World Network, 1997.

5 Global casino

The deregulation of global finance coupled with the microelectronics revolution has sparked a surge in the flow of capital. This uncontrolled speculation has eclipsed long-term productive investment and poses a huge threat to the stability of the global economy. Recent financial crises caused suffering for millions and confirm the need for urgent action to control the money markets and rein in currency traders.

THE ACCELERATION OF economic globalization is dramatically altering life for people around the world. As wealth increases for a minority of humankind, disparities between rich and poor widen and the assault on our planet's natural resources speeds up.

But the biggest and most dangerous change over the past 30 years has been in the area of global finance. The volume of worldwide foreign exchange transactions has exploded as country after country has lowered barriers to foreign investment. In 1980 the daily average of foreign exchange trading totaled $80 billion; today it is estimated that more than $1,500 billion changes hands daily on global currency markets.

That is an unimaginable sum of money, but it is all the more stunning when you realize that most of this investment has virtually nothing to do with producing real goods and services for real people. In 1998 the annual global trade in merchandise and services was $6.5 billion – equal to only 4.3 days of trading on foreign exchange markets. [1]

The world of international finance is technically arcane but essentially one-dimensional. The goal is to make money – the end-use of the investment is relevant only to the extent that it is profitable. As growth in the real economy declines due to over-capacity and shrinking wages worldwide, speculative investment has grown. Money chasing money has eclipsed productive investment as the motor of the global economy. There are very few controls on the movement of international capital. Yet the predominant view of the Bretton Woods institutions, and the giant global banks and private corporations, is that the world needs more financial liberalization, not less.

Others are not so sure. They're more inclined to believe what Keynes wrote in his 1936 book *The General Theory of Employment, Interest and Money*. 'Speculators may do no harm as bubbles on a steady stream of enterprise,' he warned, 'but the position is serious when enterprise becomes the bubble on a whirlpool of speculation.' The rules for running the global economy, laid down at Bretton Woods after World War Two, specifically sought to rein in finance capital and contain it within national borders. Keynes was Britain's delegate to the meeting and he warned that unregulated flows of international capital would remove power from elected politicians and put it into the hands of the rich investors. The ultimate allegiance of investors, he said, is to their own self-interest.

That self-interest is creating havoc today. Since global markets began to deregulate in the early 1980s, short-term speculation has become the single-largest component in the flow of international investment. Managers of billion-dollar hedge funds, mutual funds and pension plans move money in and out of countries at lightning speed based on fractional differences in exchange rates. This volatile flow of currency is almost completely detached from the physical economy. For every dollar that is needed to facilitate the trade in real goods, nine dollars is gambled in foreign exchange markets.

Critics of corporate-led globalization charge that unregulated flows of capital pose a major threat to the stability of the global economy, turning the world into a 'global financial casino'. This free flow of capital has also had a direct political impact, leaving national governments hostage to market sentiments.

Riding the whirlpool

More than $1.5 trillion ($1,500 billion) changes hands daily on global currency markets.

- The *annual* global trade in merchandise and services was $6.5 billion in 1998, the equivalent of just 4.3 days of trading on foreign exchange (forex) markets.

- Actual foreign exchange reserves in the hands of all governments in the same year totaled $1.6 trillion or just over a day's trading on forex markets.

- An estimated 95% of all forex deals are short-term speculation; more than 80% are completed in less than a week and 40% in less than two days.

- The amount of private financial flows entering poor nations exploded from $44 billion in 1990 to $256 billion in 1997. ■

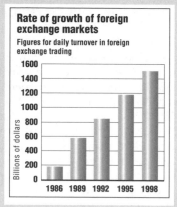

Rate of growth of foreign exchange markets

Figures for daily turnover in foreign exchange trading

Billions of dollars (y-axis: 0, 200, 400, 600, 800, 1000, 1200, 1400, 1600)

Years: 1986, 1989, 1992, 1995, 1998

The Global Gamblers, British Banks and the Foreign Exchange Game, War on Want, 1999.

Any departure from the received wisdom is instantly punished. This threat leads to a massive degree of self-censorship and a serious loss of democracy.

The development of sophisticated computerized communications, coupled with a global push for financial deregulation in the late 1970s and early 1980s were the twin sparks for an explosion of speculative investment. During the 1990s the World Bank, the IMF and the US Treasury stridently preached the benefits of liberal financial markets, pressing Third World governments to open their stock markets and financial services industries.

Ironically, the original Bretton Woods agreements specifically sought to limit the movement of finance capital and contain it within national borders. Article VI of the original IMF Articles of Agreement allows members 'to exercise such controls as are necessary to regulate international capital movements'.

Under pressure from what former advisor to the Director-General of GATT, Jagdish Bhagwati, calls the 'Wall Street/Treasury' complex, governments in the early 1980s began to dismantle national controls on both the flow of investment capital and profits across their borders. At the same time the financial services industry itself underwent an unprecedented revolution, sparking a wave of mergers, acquisitions and overseas expansion which is yet unfinished. In most countries banks, trust companies, insurance companies and investment brokerages were given the right to fight for each other's business and to compete across international borders. This level of deregulation had not been witnessed in Western countries since the depression of the 1930s.

A fully computerized global finance system means currency traders can move millions of dollars around the world instantly with a few taps on a computer keyboard. Investors instantly profit from minute fluctuations in the price of currencies. The result is what Filipino economist Walden Bello calls a game of global arbitrage 'where capital moves from one market to another, seeking to turn profits from the exploitation of the imperfections of globalized markets by taking advantage of interest-rate differentials, targeting gaps between nominal currency values and the "real" currency values, and short-selling in stocks – that is borrowing shares to artificially inflate share values, then selling.' Since volatility is central to this high-tech world of instant millions it is not surprising, says Bello, that it has also become the driving force of the global capitalist system as a whole. [2]

Besides speculating in foreign exchange markets, money managers may also plough their money into direct investment or portfolio investment. Foreign direct investment (FDI) – which tends to be stable and more long term – occurs when foreigners buy equity in local companies, when they buyout existing companies or when they actually start up a new factory or business.

Foreign portfolio investment (FPI) – which is typically more volatile – is when foreigners buy shares in the local stock market. The trouble begins because portfolio investors have few ties to bind them to the countries in which their funds are invested. In the current global system where liberalized financial markets are the norm there are no constraints to prohibit investors from selling out when they've turned a quick profit or exiting at the first signs of financial difficulties.

UNCTAD has documented the shift from FDI to FPI over the last decade. According to their 1998 *World Investment Report*, FPI accounted for a third of all private investment in developing countries from 1990 to 1997. And in some countries like Argentina, Brazil, Mexico, Thailand and South Korea portfolio investment actually outstripped direct investment. The UN agency notes that increasing FPI can signal a more volatile global economy because portfolio investors are 'attracted not so much by the prospect of long-term growth as by the prospect of immediate gain'. Thus they are prone to herd behavior which can lead to 'massive withdrawals' in a crisis.

And crises we've seen – from 1973 to 1995 there were 11 major global financial blow-ups. All of them required active intervention by international financial institutions and national governments to keep the world system from collapsing. The last major one began in Southeast Asia in mid-1997 when 'hot money' panicked and fled as quickly as it had arrived. Although the IMF and the US Government eventually stepped in with an emergency bailout of more than $120 billion, the damage from the financial chaos was widespread. Currencies were devalued in Thailand, Indonesia, the Philippines and South Korea; factories were shut down, imports slashed, workers laid off and public sector services like healthcare, education and transport cut drastically.

As the UN Development Program commented in its 1999 *Human Development Report*: 'The East Asian crisis in not an isolated accident, it is a symptom of general weakness in global capital markets.' The UN agency was not alone in its assessment. Even the stridently pro-business magazine, *The Economist*, was forced to admit that abrupt reversals in capital 'have challenged the conventional wisdom that it is a good thing to let capital move freely across borders'. Others like Jagdish Bhagwati were less equivocal. He noted that 'the Asian crisis cannot be separated from excessive borrowings of foreign short-term capital... It has become apparent that crises attendant on capital mobility cannot be ignored.'

Freefall in Southeast Asia

The Southeast Asian economy went into freefall in the summer of 1997. But in the 18 months prior to the crash more short-term investment money had entered the region than in the previous ten years. Capital inflows to Thailand and Malaysia in the 1990s amounted to more than 10 per cent of Gross Domestic Product (GDP) and most of that 'hot money' went into short-term debt. Prior to that these nations had been much more cautious about foreign investment and had taken steps to develop domestic industry by closing the door to cheaper imports from the West.

All that changed in the 1990s when these Southeast Asian countries became the star pupils of the so-called 'Washington Consensus'. Both the IMF and the World Bank had advised the countries to deregulate their capital accounts as a way of enticing foreign investment and kick-starting the development process. Starting around 1990 Thailand, Malaysia, Indonesia and the Philippines all adopted an open-door policy to foreign investment. The policy included jacking up domestic interest rates to attract portfolio investment and pegging the national currency to the dollar to ensure that foreign investors wouldn't get hit in case of sudden shifts in the value of the currency.

In one of the most thorough examinations of the

impact of 'hot money' on national economies, Walden Bello outlines the case of Thailand. In 1994 the World Bank noted in its annual report that 'Thailand provides an excellent example of the dividends to be obtained through outward orientation, receptivity to foreign investment and a market-friendly philosophy backed up by conservative macro-economic management and cautious external borrowing policies.'

Ironically, it was in Thailand that the economic boom first began to fizzle – sparked by the herd mentality of short-term investors. Bello notes that in 1992-1993 the country gave in to IMF pressure and adopted a radical deregulation of its financial system. Measures included: fewer constraints on the portfolio management of financial institutions and commercial banks; looser rules on the expansion of the business of banks and financial institutions; dismantling of foreign exchange controls; and the establishment of the Bangkok International Banking Facility (BIBF). The BIBF was a way for both local and foreign banks to take part in offshore and onshore lending. Firms licensed by the BIBF could both accept deposits and make loans in foreign currencies, to residents and non-residents. Most of the foreign capital entering the country soon came in the form of BIBF dollar loans.

Pinball capital

The problem was that the capital flooding into Thailand was neither patient nor rooted. Most of it was not invested in goods-producing industries but in areas where profits were reckoned to be sizable and quick. Millions flooded into the stock market (where the investment inflated prices beyond the value of their true worth) and into real estate and various kinds of easy consumer credit like car financing. By late 1996 there was an estimated $24 billion in 'hot money' in Bangkok alone. So much money had been pumped into Thai real estate that the value of unsold office buildings and apartments in the country nudged the

$20 billion mark. As a result of this inflow of offshore investment the country's foreign debt ballooned from $21 billion in 1988 to $89 billion in 1996. The vast majority of this – more than 80 per cent – was owed to the private sector. [3]

It was a similar story throughout the region. South Korea's foreign debt nearly tripled from $44 billion to $120 billion from 1993 to 1997 – nearly 70 per cent of that was in short-term, easily withdrawn funds. In Indonesia, companies outside the financial sector built up $40 billion in debt by the middle of 1997, 87 per cent of which was short-term. According to official figures the five countries in the region (Indonesia, Thailand, Malaysia, the Philippines and South Korea) had a combined debt to foreign banks of $274 billion just before the crisis: 64 per cent of that was in short-term obligations. This was a recipe for financial disaster.

In Thailand much of the speculative capital went into real estate, always a favorite for those with a get-rich-quick dream in mind. But it was this massive real estate bubble that finally frayed the nerves of foreign investors. When they realized that their money was tied up in property for which there were no buyers, and that Thai banks were carrying billions in bad debt that could not be serviced, foreign investors panicked and hurried to withdraw their funds. The anxiety (later dubbed the 'contagion effect') spread quickly from Thailand and Malaysia to Indonesia, the Philippines and South Korea. Like the plague this financial chaos was felt to be a contagious disease which could jump national borders. In just over a year there was a complete turnaround in the capital account of the region: in 1996 new financial inflows to the five countries totaled $93 billion. In 1997, $105 billion left those same countries – a net outflow of $12 billion. All investors rushed for the exit at the same time because none of them wanted to get caught with depreciated local currency and assets. [4]

The vicious downwards spiral picked up speed –

egged on by speculators who intervened massively in foreign exchange markets and helped seriously deval-ue local currencies. Under speculative attack the governments of the region did what they could to ward off the inevitable. The first line of defense was to raid their own foreign exchange reserves to buy up their national currency in the market, in a last-ditch attempt to maintain its value. But to no avail. Speculators continued to bail out in droves. The next step was to float their currencies but that too back-fired, proving to be a catalyst for further devaluation. So the hemorrhage from the area of foreign funds helped both to deplete foreign exchange reserves and to drive down the value of domestic currencies.

The Thai *baht* felt the pressure first but the devalu-ation soon spread to the other countries. As the currency drifted downwards, local firms who had bor-rowed from abroad had to pay more in local currency for the foreign exchange needed to service their over-seas debts. At the first sign that things were spinning out of control many foreign banks and other creditors refused to roll over their loans. They demanded imme-diate repayment. At this point the panic that gripped the region suddenly became a crisis threatening to capsize the entire global economy. Soon, internation-al financial operators were selling *baht, ringgit* and *rupiah* in an effort to cut potential losses and get their funds safely back to Europe and the US. In the ensu-ing capital flight, Asian stock prices plunged and the value of local currencies collapsed. Businesses that had taken out dollar-denominated loans couldn't afford the dollar payments to Western creditors.

For a time governments tried to stave off default by lending some of their foreign currency reserves to indebted firms. South Korea used up some $30 billion in this way. But the money soon ran out. Western banks refused to make new loans or roll over old debts. Asian businesses defaulted, cutting output and laying off workers. As the region's economies sputtered, panic intensified. Asian currencies lost 35 to 85 per cent of their foreign-exchange value, driving up prices on imported goods and pushing down the standard of living. Businesses large and small were driven to bankruptcy by the sudden drying up of credit; within a year, millions of workers had lost jobs while prices of imports, including basic foodstuffs, soared.

Calming investors

In an effort to calm investors and forestall total financial collapse the International Monetary Fund (IMF) was called in with a $120 billion bailout plan. But the IMF rescue package actually succeeded in making a bad situation worse – not least for the citizens of those nations who had to endure the impact of the Fund's edict. One of the central requirements of the package was that governments guarantee continued debt service payments to the private sector in return for the agency persuading creditors to roll over or restructure their loans. This mirrored the IMF's role during the Third World debt crisis of the 1980s. Public money from Northern taxpayers (via the Fund) was handed over to indebted governments, then recycled to commercial banks in the South to pay off their debts to private investors. In Asia this bailout of international creditors was dubbed 'socialism for the global financial élite' by some critics.

The Fund's Asian package also forced countries to further liberalize their capital account. The goal was to cut government expenditure and produce a surplus. The standard tools were applied: high interest rates combined with cuts to both government expenditures and subsidies to basics like food, fuel and transport. The high interest rates were supposed to be the bait to lure back foreign capital so all would be well again. But the bait didn't work. Tight domestic credit combined with high interest rates sparked a much sharper recession than would have otherwise taken place and did nothing to restore investor confidence.

Output in some countries fell 16 per cent or more, unemployment soared and wages nose-dived. In Thailand GDP growth-rate estimates plummeted after the IMF intervention, from 2.5 per cent in August 1997 to minus 3.5 per cent in February 1998. In Indonesia the IMF forced the Government to close down 16 banks, a move it thought would restore confidence in the notoriously inefficient banking system. Instead it led to panic withdrawals by customers at remaining banks which brought further chaos. It is estimated that half the businesses in the country went bankrupt.

The set-back for development was so severe that non-governmental agencies estimated it would take a decade or longer to make-up the lost ground. Oxfam analyzed the situation as follows:

'The crisis now gripping East Asia bears comparison in terms of its destructive impact with the Great Depression of 1929. What started as a financial crisis

Bankrolling speculation

Top global banks gambling in foreign exchange markets, by rank and estimated market share. ■

Rank 1999		%
1	Citigroup	7.75
2	Deutsche Bank	7.12
3	Chase Manhattan	7.09
4	Warburg Dillon Read	6.44
5	Goldman Sachs	4.86
6	Bank of America	4.39
7	JP Morgan	4.00
8	HSBC (Midland Bank)	3.75
9	ABN Amro	3.37
10	Merrill Lynch	3.27
11	Crédit Suisse First Boston	3.11
12	SEB	2.68
13	NatWest Global Financial Markets	2.63
14	Royal Bank of Canada	2.60
15	Morgan Stanley Dean Witter	2.29

The Global Gamblers, British Banks and the Foreign Exchange Game, War on Want, 1999.

has been allowed to develop into a full-fledged social and economic crisis, with devastating consequences for human development. Previously rising incomes have been reversed and unemployment and under-employment has reached alarming levels. Rising food prices and falling social spending have further aggravated the social conditions of the poorest.' [5]

The human impact of the crisis was stunning. According to the UN's International Labor Organization (ILO) more than 20 million people in Indonesia were laid off from September 1997 to September 1998. UNICEF said that 250,000 clinics in the country were closed and predicted that infant mortality would jump by 30 per cent. The Asian Development Bank said that more than six million children had dropped out of school. And Oxfam estimated that more than 100 million Indonesians were living in poverty a year after the crisis – four times more than two years earlier.

There was also a frightening resurgence of racial 'scape-goating' and inter-communal violence throughout the region. Malaysia's autocratic leader Mahathir Mohamad blamed Jewish financiers for destabilizing his Muslim country, while in Indonesia the shops of ethnic-Chinese merchants were looted and burned and hundreds of Chinese brutally beaten and killed.

There were, however, some clear winners that emerged from the Asian meltdown. The big ones were the Western corporate interests that rushed in to snap up the region's bargain-basement assets after the economic collapse. As former US Trade Representative Mickey Kantor said at the time, the recession in the 'Tiger Economies' was a golden chance for the West to 'reassert' its commercial interests. 'When countries seek help from the IMF,' he said, 'Europe and America should use the IMF as a battering ram to gain advantage.' [6]

That was certainly true in South Korea where the IMF agreement lifted restrictions on outside ownership so that foreigners could purchase up to 55 per cent of Korean companies and 100 per cent of Korean banks. Years of effort by the Korean élite to keep businesses firmly under control of state-supported conglomerates called *chaebols* were undone in a matter of months. In January 1998 the French investment firm Credit Lyonnais estimated that just 87 of the country's 653 non-financial firms were safe from foreign buyers. Rudi Dornbusch, a US economist, accurately summed up the overall impact of the economic crisis. 'Korea is now owned and operated by our Treasury,' he crowed. 'That's the positive side of this crisis.' [7]

A key reason why the Asian economies were so vulnerable to currency destabilization was that they had gradually abandoned controls over the movement of capital. When a country cedes its control over capital flows it effectively removes any tools it may have for intervening in the market process, leaving itself at the mercy of speculators whose only concern is profit. More critically, nations lose the ability to control internal economic strategies which lie at the heart of national sovereignty. How can a nation hope to determine its own social agenda and economic future if key policy areas are shaped by the self-interest of foreign investors and money markets?

At the time of the Asian meltdown, one country emerged from the chaos in noticeably better shape than the others. Although Malaysia's GDP fell by 7.5 per cent in 1998, the nation managed to escape the devastating social impact felt elsewhere. Partly this was because Malaysia adopted a range of defensive measures to limit capital flight, many of which were modeled on the Chinese example. The Malaysian Central Bank ruled that private companies could only contract foreign loans if they could show that the loans would end up producing foreign exchange which then could be used to service the debt. And like China, Malaysia also pegged its currency, the *ringgit*, to the US dollar and allowed it to be freely converted to other foreign currencies for trade and direct invest-ment. However, portfolio investors had to keep their funds inside Malaysia for a minimum of one year and residents were restricted in how much money they could take out of the country.

Most importantly, trade in *ringgit* outside the coun-try was not recognized by the Government and this helped to prevent manipulation by currency specula-tors. Measures were also taken to stop investment from beyond the country's borders coming into the Malaysian stock market. The controls allowed the Malaysian Government to stimulate the domestic economy with tax cuts, lower interest rates and spend-ing on public infrastructue – without having to worry about speculators targeting its currency. Interest rates fell from 11 to 7 per cent, a helpful boon to local busi-nesses and the domestic banking industry.

China's response

Despite its authoritarian political structure China was also able to sidestep the Asian trap – mainly by avoid-ing becoming entangled in international financial markets. As a result China has considerably more con-trol over its domestic economy than just about any nation in the world. Its currency, the *renmimbi*, is not freely convertible; its finance system is more or less domestically owned and controlled by the State and there is still relatively little foreign investment in the Chinese stock market. Plus the world's biggest nation was not then a member of the IMF or the WTO – though full membership in the WTO is imminent.

As a result China was not vulnerable to the specula-tive herd behavior that devastated other countries in the region. Instead of devaluing its currency and try-ing to grab a share of its neighbors' exports, China took another tack. The Government decided to direct national savings into a $200 billion public works pro-gram to stimulate its domestic economy. [8]

Chile is another example of a country that successfully tried to regulate destabilizing short-term flows of foreign capital by installing a series of financial 'speed bumps' to slow down speculation. When Mexico's economy crashed in 1995 Chile was able to escape the worse 'contagion' effects because of its *encaje* policy. This government regulation required foreign investors to deposit funds equivalent to 30 per cent of their investment in Chile's central bank. In addition, portfolio investors were required to keep their cash inside the country for a minimum of at least a year. These barriers slowed down the exodus of funds from Chile and kept it from falling victim to what the financial press dubbed Mexico's 'tequila effect'.

Market buzz

A pocket guide to the language of the financial market place.

• **Hedging**

If a business holds stocks of a commodity like cocoa or copper it runs the risk of losing money if the price falls before it can unload it all. This loss can be avoided by 'hedging' the risk. This involves selling the item before the purchaser actually wants it – i.e. for delivery at an agreed price at a future date. Hedge funds make a business of selling and buying this risk, often using borrowed money to put together 'highly leveraged' deals. The most infamous hedge fund, the US firm, Long Term Capital Management (LTCM), had to be rescued with a $3.5 billion bailout from other Wall Street investment companies after it overextended itself to the tune of $200 billion. The firm had invested $500 million of borrowed money for every million dollars it invested of its own cash.

• **Futures, options and swaps**

A futures contract is an agreement to buy or sell a commodity or shares or currency at a future date at a price decided when the contract is first agreed. An option is like a futures contract except that in this case there is a right, but no obligation, to trade at an agreed price at a future date. An interest-rate swap is a transaction by which financial institutions change the form of their assets or debts. Swaps can be between fixed and floating rate debt, or between debt in different currencies.

• **Derivatives**

A sweeping, catchall term used to refer to a range of extremely complex and obscure financial arrangements. Futures contracts, futures on stock market indices, options and swaps are all derivatives. In general, derivatives are tradable securities whose value is 'derived' (thus the name) from some underlying instrument which may be a stock, bond, commodity or currency. They can be used as a hedge to reduce risks or for speculation.

Shaken by the Asian débâcle Western finance ministers, led by the US, came up with a new plan to aid countries experiencing balance-of-payments shortfalls before such a crisis occurs. The idea was to give more money (up to $90 billion) and more power to the IMF to create 'an enhanced IMF facility for countries pursuing strong IMF-approved policies'. The thinking was that an instant loan from a 'precautionary fund' would make currency speculators less anxious and so tame the 'hot money' and stall a devaluation.

Brazil was the first country to use the new IMF plan. Unfortunately, Brazil's economy seemed no more immune to financial crisis than Indonesia or Thailand.

The notional value of all derivatives in effect in 1999 was $90 trillion which dwarfs the value of all the world's stock markets combined.

• **Stock market indices**

The most famous are the Dow Jones Industrial Average, an index of share prices on the US stock market based on 30 leading US companies, the FTSE 100, an index of Britain's 100 top companies and the Japanese equivalent, the NIKKEI 225.

• **Foreign exchange market**

This is where currencies are traded. There is no single location for this market since it operates via computer and telephone connections in an interlaced web linking hundreds of trading points all over the world. The total turnover of world foreign exchange markets is enormous, many times the total international trade in goods and services.

• **Mutual funds/Unit trusts**

A financial institution which holds shares on behalf of investors. The investors buy shares or 'units' in the fund, which uses their money to buy shares in a range of companies. An investor selling back the units gets the proceeds of selling a fraction of the fund's total portfolio rather than just shares in one or two companies.

• **Equities**

The ordinary shares or common stock of companies. The owners of these shares are entitled to the residual profits of companies after all claims of creditors, debenture holders and preference shareholders have been satisfied. These are paid out to stock owners in the form of dividends.

• **Junk bonds**

Bonds issued on very doubtful security by firms where there is serious doubt as to whether interest and redemption payments will actually be made. Because these bonds are so risky, lenders are only prepared to hold them if promised returns are high enough. ■

When the Brazilian *real* first came under attack in 1998 the government of Fernando Cardoso spent more than $40 billion in foreign exchange trying to prop it up. Cardoso also raised domestic interest rates to 50 per cent to try to keep capital from fleeing the country. Nevertheless traders continued to hammer the *real* even after the country signed a formal letter of intent with the IMF. By January 1999 nearly a billion dollars a day was exiting the country – the Government had no choice but to finally devalue its currency which lost nearly a third of its value overnight.

Brazilian crash

Meanwhile, the Brazilian economy was crashing as IMF policies kicked in. High interest rates scared off domestic business owners who could no longer afford to borrow. Budget cuts and public sector layoffs increased poverty and unemployment as the Government was forced to implement what the IMF called 'the largest privatization program in history'. As in Asia the IMF/US Treasury plan highlighted foreign investment as Brazil's only long-term hope, despite the fact that each percentage increase in domestic interest rates adds millions to debt service costs, all of which has to be repaid in hard currencies purchased with the devalued Brazilian *real*. By the end of 1999 Brazil's total external debt, always the highest in the South, topped more than $230 billion.

Despite the obvious danger of capital ricocheting around the globe, the IMF and the US Treasury have been reluctant to support mechanisms to inhibit its movement. And speculators themselves have also been working overtime to squelch defensive government action against their attacks. Pressures to lift exchange controls have increased despite repeated crises and heavy criticism.

Noted free-trade advocate Jagdish Bhagwati argues that lax capital controls serve the 'self-interest' of financiers by enlarging the area in which they can make money. 'The ideology of free trade has been hijacked by the proponents of capital mobility,' he says bluntly. [9]

The original Bretton Woods agreement did not fulfill Keynes' dream of giving 'every member government the explicit right to control capital movements' but the policies did give members some controls. Unfortunately, even these limited tools have been gradually eroded over the years by the growing insistence on deregulation. US Treasury official Lawrence Summers criticized efforts by Malaysia, Hong Kong and others to hobble the movement of overseas capital. He called controls a 'catastrophe' and urged countries to 'open up to foreign financial service providers, and all the competition, capital and expertise they bring with them'. Given the damage inflicted on millions by the fickle nature of short-term speculators, Summers' fundamentalism comes across as both short-sighted and harmful.

As people from Mexico to Russia see their lives wrecked by the whipsaw effect of one global financial crisis after another it is becoming painfully evident that the old ways no longer work. The world has been led to the brink of financial chaos too often in the last decade. Solutions are needed urgently to ensure that money markets, bond traders and currency speculators are brought under the control of national governments in the interest of the public good.

1 *The Global Gamblers, British Banks and the Foreign Exchange Game*, War on Want, London, 1999; 2 'Domesticating Markets: A social justice perspective on the debate over a new global financial architecture', by Walden Bello, *Multinational Monitor*, March 1999; 3 Testimony of Walden Bello before the House Banking Committee, US House of Representatives, April 21, 1998; 4 *Human Development Report 1999*, UN Development Program/Oxford University Press; 5 Oxfam *East Asia Briefing*, available from www.oxfam.org.uk/policy/eabrief; 6 Quoted in 'Globalization for Whom?', Mark Weisbrot, Research Director, Preamble Center, www.preamble.org/globalization; 7 Quoted in 'Asian Crisis Spurs Search for New Global Rules', *Economic Justice Report*, July 1998; 8 'The Case for National Economic Sovereignty', Mark Weisbrot, Third World Network Features, July 1999; 9 'The Capital Myth: the difference between the trade in widgets and the trade in dollars', Jagdish Bhagwati, *Foreign Affairs*, May/June 1998.

6 Poverty, the environment and the market

Faith in economic growth as the key to progress comes into question as the Earth's life-support systems fray and signs of ecological collapse multiply. Globalization geared to spur rapid growth through greater resource consumption is straining the environment and widening gaps between rich and poor. The standard cure of neo-liberal economics – privatization, tax cuts and foreign investment – is not effective. Criticism and concern grows from both expert-insiders and grassroots communities.

WHETHER THEY ARE disciples of Keynes, confirmed free-marketers or Stalinist central planners, economists of all stripes have an abiding faith in the healing powers of economic growth. Keynesians opt for government regulation and an active fiscal policy to kick-start spending in times of slow growth. They believe the impact of state spending will catalyze the general economy, create jobs and stimulate consumption. Keynesians and those on the Left in general have been more concerned with making sure that the growing pie was distributed fairly. And they have held out for more control over the production process by workers themselves.

Neo-liberals hope to boost consumption using different levers. They opt for 'pure' market solutions – tax cuts and low interest rates – both of which are supposed to increase spending and investment by putting more money into peoples' pockets.

But, until recently, all sides have ignored the environment. The increasingly global economy is completely dependent on the larger economy of the planet Earth. And evidence is all around us that the planet's ecological health is in trouble.

Our system of industrial production has chewed

through massive quantities of non-renewable natural resources over the past two centuries. Not only are we wiping out ecosystems and habitats at an alarming rate, but it is also clear that we are exploiting our natural resource base (the economy's 'natural capital') and generating waste at a rate which exceeds the capacity of the natural world to regenerate and heal itself.

We don't have to look far for proof that growth-centered economics is pushing the regenerative capacities of the planet's ecosystems to the brink. The worry is not the one raised by the Club of Rome's report *Limits to Growth* more than 20 years ago. There is no immediate shortage of non-renewable resources. Even at current rates of consumption there is enough copper, iron and nickel to last centuries. More pressing is the disintegration of the basic life-support systems that we take for granted. The water cycle, the composition of the atmosphere, the assimilation of waste and recycling of nutrients, the pollination of crops, the delicate interplay of species: all these are in danger.

There is now a large body of research documenting this precipitous decline. Deserts are spreading, forests being hacked down, fertile soils ruined by erosion and desalinization, fisheries exhausted and ground water reserves pumped dry. Carbon dioxide levels in the atmosphere continue to rise due to our extravagant burning of fossil fuels. In September 1995 the Intergovernmental Panel on Climate Change, a select group of nearly 2,500 of the world's top climate scientists, concluded that climate change is unstoppable and will lead to 'widespread economic, social and environmental dislocation over the next century'.

The World Conservation Union's (IUCN) 2000 Red List of Threatened Species warns that the global extinction crisis is accelerating, with dramatic declines in populations of many species, including reptiles and primates. The Swiss-based IUCN sees habitat loss, human exploitation and invasion by alien species as major threats to wildlife. This loss of habitat is affecting 89 per cent of all threatened birds, 83 per cent of threatened mammals and 91 per cent of threatened plants. The highest number of threatened mammals and birds are found in lowland and mountain tropical rain forests where over 900 bird species and 55 per cent of all mammals are threatened. In the last 500 years, human activity has forced 816 species to extinction. Scientists reckon the normal extinction rate is one species every four years. Today's die-off rate is estimated at 1,000 to 10,000 times the natural rate. [1]

Stealing from the future

Since 1950 global economic output has jumped from $3.8 trillion to $18.9 trillion, a nearly five-fold increase. We have consumed more of the world's natural capital in this brief period than during the entire history of humankind.

The ecologist and economist William Rees estimates that around 10-14 acres (4-6 hectares) of land are used to maintain the consumption of the average person in the West. But he says the total available productive land in the world is about 4.25 acres (1.7 hectares) per person (total land divided by population). The difference Rees calls 'appropriated carrying capacity' – which basically means the rich are living off the resources of the poor.

The Netherlands, for example, consumes the output of a productive land mass 14 times its size. Most Northern countries and many urban regions in the South already consume more than their fair share; they depend on trade (using someone else's natural assets) or on depleting their own natural capital. Such regions, says Rees, 'run an unaccounted ecological deficit – their population either appropriating carrying capacity from elsewhere or from future generations'. [2]

Faith in economic growth as the ultimate hope for human progress is widespread. A central tenet of economists on the Left and Right has been that the 'carrying capacity' of the Earth is infinitely expandable. The belief is that a combination of ingenuity and technology will eventually allow us all to live like middle-class Americans – if only we can only ignore the naysayers and keep the economy growing.

Unfortunately, reality shows otherwise. Says ecologist Robert Ayres: 'There is every indication that human economic activity supported by perverse trade and growth policies is well on the way to perturbing our natural environment more and faster than any known event in planetary history, save perhaps the large asteroid collision that may have killed off the dinosaurs. We may well be on the way to our own extinction.' [3]

Ayres is correct when he accuses globalization of accelerating the process of global environmental decline. Export-led growth and Third World debt have combined to speed up the rapid consumption of the Earth's irreplaceable natural resources. Some environmentalists argue that primary resources (nature's goods and services) are too cheap and that their price does not reflect either their finite nature or the hidden social and ecological costs of extraction. To conserve resources we have to make them more expensive. There is some truth to this, especially since world-market prices for raw materials – commodities like timber, sugar, coffee, copper and, until recently, oil – have never been lower.

Prices plummeted during the Asian financial crisis. But debt in the South, the source of many of the world's commodities, has also kept prices low. 'Adjustment' policies imposed by the IMF/World Bank as the price of admission to the global trading community mean that poor countries are obliged to service their debts before they are allowed to do anything else. Their only option is to expand raw material exports to world markets.

And therein lies the problem. Because all poor countries have to increase their exports at once, there is a glut and prices fall – sometimes by half. So that twice as much has to be exported to earn the same amount of foreign currency. The beneficiaries are the rich countries and Western-based corporations. They not only get their debts serviced, but cheap commodities keep prices down, profits up and inflation under control in the North. The losers are the people of the South – and the global environment.

Deregulated destruction

Globalization policies put the squeeze on the environment in other ways, too. Take the case of Brazil which environmentalists consider one of the Earth's most ecologically important nations. The country still contains 30 per cent of the planet's rainforest long considered to be 'the lungs of the world'. Scientists believe the spectacular biological diversity of the rainforest is a potential cornucopia of priceless, life-saving drugs.

In 1999 the Brazilian Government slashed millions of dollars off environmental spending in the wake of IMF-enforced cuts. The country's environmental enforcement arm had its budget reduced by 19 per cent. In addition the domestic recession brought on by IMF policies boosted unemployment, forcing many ordinary workers and peasants to clear larger areas of jungle for subsistence.

Gustavo Fonseca of the Center for Biological Science at the Washington-based Conservation International sums up the concern of environmentalists: 'Our biggest worry now is that the Government is going to lose control of attempts to control deforestation. This is undermining the very basis of what we've been trying to accomplish in Brazil.' [4]

In Asia, even before the crash of 1997, the region's 'economic miracle' had been built on a fast-track liquidation of its natural resources. Pristine rainforests were plundered, rivers despoiled, seacoasts poisoned with pesticides and fisheries exhausted. In the Indonesian capital, Jakarta, more than 70 per cent of water samples were found to be 'highly contaminated by chemical pollutants' while the country's forests were being hacked down at the rate of 6 million acres (2.4 million hectares) per year. In the Malaysian state of Sarawak (part of the island of Borneo) 30 per cent of the forest disappeared in a mere two decades, while in peninsular Malaysia 73 per cent of 116 rivers surveyed by authorities were found to be either 'biologically dead' or 'dying'. [5]

The respected international environmental group, Friends of the Earth (FoE), summarized the impact of free-market deregulation on Third World environments in its recent study *IMF: Selling the Environment Short.* 'Decreased spending weakens a government's ability to enforce environmental laws and diminishes efforts to promote conservation. Budget priorities are often directed towards business promotion, creating a further strain on cash-strapped environmental enforcement agencies.'

The persistence of poverty has also spurred environmental decline – the desperately poor do not make good eco-citizens. Tribal peoples plunder the forest on which they depend for survival; animals are poached and slaughtered by impoverished African villagers for their valuable ivory or their body parts.

In Madagascar, one of the world's most devastated environments, an island once covered in lush forests has turned into a barren wasteland as local people slash-and-burn jungle plots to grow food. In a few short years the land turns to scrub-infested desert and the people continue their cycle of cutting and burning. Less than a tenth of Madagascar is still tree-covered and the forest is vanishing at the rate of 500,000 acres (200,000 hectares) a year. Poverty is the core of the problem: 70 per cent of the island's 14 million people live on less than a dollar a day. [1]

The logic of globalization is seductive because it is based on a simple principle: free the market of constraints and its self-evolving dynamic will bring employment, wealth and prosperity. But despite the confidence of those who preach the neo-liberal gospel, there are clear indications that people are losing their faith.

The signs are inescapable – not least of all are the thousands of civil society groups around the world who have begun to take their protests to the streets. More than 50,000 people from dozens of countries gathered in Seattle in November 1999 at the annual meeting of the World Trade Organization. The gathering was a unique mix of environmentalists, trade unionists, peasant groups, students and ordinary citizens – all united by their concern that economic globalization is spinning out of control. Then in April 2000 another 15,000 protesters gathered in Washington for a repeat attack on the IMF and the World Bank at their spring meetings. Ironically, as if to prove the protesters' point, stock markets nose-dived the same week when a wave of panic-selling swept the globe, puncturing the high-tech stock bubble that had carried markets to dizzying new heights. And in Prague in October 2000 the two agencies again ran into a similar phalanx of protesters.

Cracks in the consensus

Even in mainstream circles globalization is coming under increasing scrutiny. The financial crises in Russia, Asia and Latin America in the last half of the 1990s opened deep rifts in the dominant 'Washington consensus' – a view which had been advocated by the Bretton Woods institutions and endorsed by Western governments. Powerful voices who had previously been amongst the most solid backers of unfettered global markets began to speak out.

The influential Harvard economist Jeffrey Sachs was one of those. He had been an advisor to the IMF, one of the main engineers of capitalist 'shock therapy' in Russia after the fall of the Soviet Union – and a leading voice in favor of economic globalization. The Asian débâcle forced him to re-examine his faith in the supremacy of free markets and to question some of the conventional solutions to national financial crises – especially the role of the IMF. He criticized the Fund for 'bad diagnosis, bad prescription and failed programs'.

In a candid *Financial Times* article published in December 1997 Sachs called the IMF 'secretive' and 'unaccountable'. 'It defies logic,' he said, that 'a small group of 1,000 economists on 19th Street in Washington should dictate the economic conditions of life to 75 developing countries with around 1.4 billion people'.

Others began to speak out too. The former World Bank executive, Joseph Stiglitz, became a much-quoted 'ex-insider' willing to publicly criticize the neo-liberal worldview. Stiglitz left his position at the World Bank as chief economist and senior vice-president at the end of 1999. The 'Washington Consensus,' he said in the April 2000 issue of *Multinational Monitor* was: 'faulty in its narrow economic strategies, but also excessively narrow in its objectives. It focused mainly on increasing GDP, not on broader concepts of increasing living standards or democratic, equitable, sustainable development.'

As if to reinforce this assessment of spreading 'economic insecurity' the IMF's *World Economic Outlook* report for 2000 noted that despite the spectacular economic growth of the past half century, the quality of life for a fifth of the world's population has actually regressed in relative, and sometimes absolute, terms. The IMF's deputy research director Flemming Larson called this spreading poverty in the midst of economic growth 'one of the greatest economic failures of the 20th century'.

One of the most cogent critiques of the downside of globalization came from the UN Development Program in its 1999 *Human Development Report.* 'When the market goes too far in dominating social and political outcomes, the opportunities and rewards of globalization spread unequally and inequitably – concentrating power and wealth in a select group of people, nations and corporations, marginalizing the others.'

The UN agency backed its analysis with hard-hitting figures on what it called a 'grotesque and dangerous polarization' between those people and countries benefiting from the system and those that are merely 'passive recipients' of its effects.

Even on its own terms economic globalization is not working. In 1960, the fifth of the world's people who live in the richest countries had 30 times more income than the fifth living in the poorest countries. By 1997 the income gap had more than doubled to 74:1. Income inequalities within countries have also increased over the past two decades. Another UN study, this one on income inequality in OECD countries, concluded that in the 1980s real wages (adjusted for inflation) had fallen and income inequality increased in all countries except Germany and Italy.

The widening gap

In the US the top ten per cent of families increased their average income by 16 per cent during that decade, while the top five per cent increased theirs by 23 per cent and the top one per cent by a whopping 50 per cent. This trend was echoed elsewhere. In Latin America the top 10 per cent of wage-earners increased their share of total income by 10 per cent while the poorest 10 per cent saw their income drop by 15 per cent, wiping out what meager improvements they had made in the previous decade. Income inequality also grew in Thailand, Indonesia, China and other Asian nations even though the region enjoyed healthy economic growth throughout the decade. In sub-Saharan Africa the situation was worse: after two decades of IMF and World Bank structural adjustment not only is income inequality growing but average per capita incomes are falling. They are now lower than they were in 1970.

This shift in wealth and income from bottom to top is part of the logic of globalization. In order to be 'competitive' governments adopt policies which cut taxes and favor profits over wages. The economic argument is simple: putting more money into the pockets of corporations and wealthy individuals (who benefit most from tax cuts: the higher the income the greater the gain) will lead to greater investment, jobs, economic growth and good times for all.

Unfortunately, there is no evidence that improvements in public well-being result from tax cuts for the rich or lower wages for the rest of us. If tax cuts were directed towards those at the bottom of the income ladder there might be some impact since the money would almost certainly be spent on basic necessities. But this isn't part of the globalization game plan. In every country that has taken up the 'reduce-taxes-cut-the-deficit' mantra the majority of tax cuts benefit wealthy individuals and corporations. What happens to the money is perhaps predictable: some goes into high-priced consumer baubles – a phenomenon which is glaringly visible amongst the élite in cities from Bangkok to Los Angeles. But most winds up in the stock market or in other sorts of non-productive speculative activity.

Major players are no longer satisfied with modest profits on long-term investment, especially when double-digit returns are available by gambling in currency speculation or derivatives. This diversion of capital away from socially-useful investment is one of the major forces fueling the 'casino economy' and the high-tech stock bubble in the US and Europe. That and the fact that investment opportunities in the goods-producing sector are shrinking due to the problem of 'over-capacity' – too many goods chasing too few buyers (see chapter 5). Computerized robots and automated assembly lines replace workers with new technology, leaving fewer people to actually buy products that factories are churning out. Those that remain find their wages under constant downward pressure in the face of cheaper labor elsewhere. The drive to be 'competitive' ends up being a race to the bottom. Workers who don't lose their jobs find their wages squeezed.

In Canada, a country which normally tops UNDP's 'human development' rankings, a recent study found that the real disposable income on average fell by 3.3 per cent between 1989 and 1999. This coincided exactly with a period of neo-liberal economic policies including drastic cuts in government expenditures, reduced taxes and relatively high domestic interest rates.

'Families have had to work longer and longer hours in order to maintain the same level of earnings from employment and the idea of an affluent leisure society made possible by technological progress has become little more than a bad joke,' concluded a report published by the Canadian Center for Policy Alternatives.

Despite these worrying warning signs, neo-liberals are reluctant to abandon their beliefs: 'Give the private sector the resources,' they say, 'and it will do the job.' But the proof is hard to find. Surplus capital which doesn't get funneled into currency markets zips straight into overseas tax havens where both rich individuals and globe-trotting multinationals have been squirreling away their cash for decades.

There are nearly 70 tax havens scattered around the world. These 'offshore financial centers' include places like the Bahamas, the Cayman Islands, Liberia and Bermuda. Investors can store their wealth secretly, no questions asked – thus escaping any social obligations to the country where they may have earned it. Only a small number of these tax havens have public disclosure laws effecting the banks which operate within their borders.

The Economist recently estimated that the 1.2 per cent of the world population who live in tax havens produce about 3 per cent of the global GDP. These countries account for 26 per cent of the world's financial assets and more than 30 per cent of the profits of

US multinationals. This final figure gives a clear sense of how important tax havens are to the corporate world. But it also underlines the flawed reasoning of those who support economic policies premised on tax cuts and corporate deregulation. In almost all cases corporations will do whatever they can to avoid paying taxes. Private companies exist to maximize returns on the investment of their stockholders – they jeopardize their own survival to the extent that they are unable to reach that goal.

This tension between the corporate world view and the broader public interest is one reason why tax havens are now coming under intense scrutiny. Countries in the Organization of Economic Cooperation and Development (OECD) and in the European Union have long recognized these havens as a drain on national treasuries and a convenient way of 'laundering' illegal funds. It is estimated that up to

Human Development Report, UN Development Program (Oxford University Press, 1992); cited in When Corporations Rule The World, David C Korten (Kumarian Press, 1995)

Mind the gap

Despite an apparent increase in global growth and steadily increasing per capita income, the gap both within and between rich and poor countries is widening.

Share of global income over time

Year	Richest 20%	Poorest 20%	Ratio of Rich/Poor
1960	70.2	2.3	30:1
1970	73.9	2.3	32:1
1980	76.3	1.7	45:1
1989	82.7	1.4	59:1
1997	90.0	1.0	74:1

• In 1960 the richest fifth of the world's population received 70% of global income compared to 2.3% for the world's poorest 20%. By 1989 the richest 20% had increased their share to 82.7% while the bottom fifth's share of global income shrank from 2.3% to 1.4%.

• In Brazil the richest 20% earn 28 times as much as the poorest 20%. In the US from 1977-89 the average real income of the top 1% increased by 78% while the poorest 20% of the population saw their income decrease by 10.4%. ■

$500 billion from the global narcotics trade passes through tax havens annually. But there is now fear that the rise of electronic commerce combined with global financial liberalization will trigger an even greater flow of wealth and profits to these tax-free enclaves. [6]

While the stock market booms and the e-commerce revolution churns out scores of dot.com millionaires, the social fabric which is the backdrop to all our lives continues to fray. This is the hidden human cost of 'market discipline' and it is as much a dilemma for European social democracies as it is for countries in Africa or Latin America.

All of us in the industrialized nations can chronicle the gradual decline in public services and social provision that has accompanied the attempt to control the deficit which is demanded by international markets. As corporate profits boom and real wages stagnate, the glue that holds us together is losing its strength. We're told there is no longer enough money to pay for 'public goods'. In exchange for a few hundred dollars in tax cuts we sacrifice our schools, reduce state support for community parks and recreation facilities, hobble our public transport and weaken our healthcare system.

In Western Europe, Canada, Australia and New Zealand (Aotearoa) public education and healthcare systems have seen repeated budget cuts as the state retreats and makes way for private, profit-oriented ventures. Welfare and unemployment benefits have been 'rationalized', slashing the number of those eligible. Senior citizens and those nearing retirement are fearful that promised pensions will evaporate as governments become more desperate for funds. Individuals are frantically scraping together whatever savings they have and heading towards the stock market in the hope that they too will ride to old-age security on the coattails of the FTSE, the Nasdaq and the Dow Jones. Government funding for the arts and for environmental protection has also been steadily eroded. This failure to protect these 'public goods' diminishes us all, makes us less capable of caring for each other and prohibits us from advancing together as a cohesive, mutually supportive community.

Globalization has also derailed development in the South where the poor continue to pay the highest price of adjustment. In order to boost exports and maintain their obligations to creditors, developing countries must divert money away from things like healthcare, education and aid to small-scale farmers. There have been countless studies detailing the social impact of structural adjustment and the findings are depressingly similar. Those with the least suffer the most.

Recent events in Brazil are typical. As the country's economy lurched into crisis in 1998 the IMF insisted on huge government cuts approaching a fifth of the budget. More than eight million of Brazil's poorest depend on subsidized rations of beans, rice and sugar for survival. The Government was forced to cut expenditures on those rations by more than half. At the same time the subsidy on school lunches was cut by 35 per cent. The 1999 budget for land reform, one of the most pressing social issues in Latin America, was reduced by 43 per cent.

Indian liberalization

The Indian Government launched its campaign to liberalize the economy and open it up to foreign investors in 1992 and opposition has been growing ever since. A 1997 Gallup poll found that two out of three Indians believed their standard of living had fallen or stagnated since embracing globalization. Demonstrations have erupted across the country as farmers worry about cheap food imports wiping out local producers. Two influential coalitions uniting hundreds of grassroots organizations are spearheading the protests. The National Alliance of Peoples' Movements is made up of more than 200 citizens' groups and was formed in 1993. The Joint Forum of Indian People Against Globalization (JAFIP) brought together more than 50 farmers and peasant groups in 1998 to demand that India withdraw from the WTO.[7]

The litany of suffering and chaos spawned by harsh market reforms is repeated across the developing world. A 1999 joint study by the Washington-based Development Gap and Friends of the Earth confirmed this damage in five different poor countries.

In Senegal, which has endured 20 years of IMF programs, the report found 'declining quality in education and health' combined with a growth in 'maternal mortality, unemployment and child labor'. In Tanzania the research found that globalization had successfully redirected agriculture towards exports but had also 'expanded rural poverty, income inequality and environmental degradation'. Food security decreased, housing conditions deteriorated and primary-school enrolment dropped while malnutrition and infant mortality rose.

In Mexico the report noted that globalization led to 'economic depression'. Millions of farmers were pushed out of agriculture and thousands of small businesses went bankrupt – 'drastically slashing jobs and wages' in the process. In Nicaragua, whose mildly leftist Sandinista government was destabilized by the US in the 1980s, IMF policies drove the country into further poverty. Financial deregulation attracted capital to 'short-term, high-interest deposits' and 'away from productive investment in small-scale domestic agriculture and manufacturing'. In Hungary, the IMF advised introducing liberalized trade, a tight money supply and rapid privatization of state assets. But the report found the policies deflected money away from education and social services and into the wallets of wealthy bond holders.

But it was in Russia that the orthodox prescription for economic reform did some of its greatest harm. Supported by billions in Western aid, subsidized loans and rescheduled debt, the plan was to turn Russia into a capitalist success story overnight. Instead the 'shock therapy' threw the economy open to the winds of corruption. Privatized state assets ended up in the hands of a small group of powerful insiders (often the same people who ran the former communist state apparatus) while ordinary Russians were saddled with colossal debts. At the same time an estimated $150 billion left the country, most of it permanently.

Poverty in Russia

In the absence of price controls and the guaranteed employment of the Soviet era, average Russians endured poverty unknown for decades. It is estimated that 70 per cent of Russians now live below the poverty line while capital investment is barely 10 per cent of what it was in 1990. The country has experienced the steepest fall in peacetime living standards in modern history. According to the UN inequality doubled from 1989 to 1996. The income share of the richest 20 per cent of Russians is 11 times that of the poorest 20 per cent. Much of the economy has returned to barter while male life expectancy dropped from 65 to 60 years (two years less than the average for developing countries) and the under-five child mortality rate jumped to 25 per thousand live births – the same as Libya or Venezuela. [8]

In all countries touched by economic globalization, women tend to bear a disproportionate share of the costs. One feminist critique of structural adjustment documented several dozen ways in which women become 'shock absorbers' for economic reforms. These include: forcing more women into 'informal' sector jobs as mainstream employment opportunities fade; promoting export crops which men tend to dominate; disrupting girls' education; increasing mortality rates and worsening female health; more incidents of domestic violence and stress; and an overall increase in the work load of women both inside and outside the home. [9]

Since women are the caregivers in most societies they tend to pick up the pieces when the social safety net is slashed. A 1997 Zimbabwe study found that 15 years of economic reform had a devastating impact on women in that southern African country. When school fees were raised, girls dropped out first and when health spending was cut by a third, the number of women dying in childbirth doubled. As male breadwinners are laid off, women do what they can to compensate for the lost income. They brew beer, turn to prostitution or become street traders. It is assumed that women will simply pick up the slack when governments cut education, healthcare and other social programs.[9]

Are the costs of growth too great? As the victims of globalization multiply, more and more people are beginning to feel the downside of the world economy. Citizens, ordinary workers, students, women, small farmers and environmentalists have begun to speak out forcefully against an economic system which they see as both harmful and unjust.

Instead of a homogenized global culture shaped by the narrow demands of the 'money economy' there is a resurgent push for equity and sustainability. Instead of a deregulated globalization which rides roughshod over the rights of nation states and communities, civil society groups from Chile to China are calling for a radical restructuring. The aim is for an economic system more connected to real human needs and aspirations – and less geared to the anti-human machinations of the corporate-led free market. In the next chapter we'll look at how we might get there.

1 *The Globe and Mail*, Toronto, April 15, 2000; **2** *Our Ecological Footprint: reducing human impact on human health*, Mathis Wackernagel and William Rees, New Society Publishers, 1996; **3** Quoted in *The global economy is a doomsday machine*, Kalle Lasn, see www.adbusters.org/campaigns/economic-globaldoomsday.html; **4** 'Brazil's sick economy infects the ecosystem', Anthony Faiola, *Guardian Weekly*, April 25, 1999; **5** 'The end of the miracle', Walden Bello, *Multinational Monitor*, Jan/Feb 1998; **6** 'No mean feat to crack down on tax havens', Madelaine Drohan, *The Globe and Mail*, Toronto, April 12, 2000; **7** 'The meek fight for their inheritance', Katharine Ainger, *Guardian Weekly*, Feb 12, 1999; **8** 'Robbing Russia', *The Nation*, October 4, 1999; **9** *Mortgaging women's lives*, P Sparr, Zed Press, 1994.

7 Redesigning the global economy

Globalization is increasing inequality and poverty worldwide as national governments lose the ability to control their development strategies and policies. Political solutions are needed to reinvigorate democratic control both North and South. But political reforms need to be combined with particular mechanisms for structural reform. In combination these should put meaningful employment and human rights at the heart of economic policy, boost local control and decision-making, and restore the ecological health and natural capital of our planet.

THE LAST SIX chapters of this book have sketched a sweeping overview of both the history and the current reality of the global economy. We've tried to show that corporate-led globalization is a juggernaut, driven by greed and notions of economic efficiency, which is radically altering social relationships, impoverishing millions of our fellow humans, stripping age-old cultures of their self-identity and threatening the environmental health of the Earth.

There is no doubt that globalization is powerful and the forces behind it are formidable. But it is not inevitable. The economic systems and structures which shape the global systems of production and distribution are human-made. The institutions which make the rules which govern the operation of the world economy are human-made. The governments which we elect are people like us who are there to represent the interests of all citizens, at least in theory. Change is possible. Indeed, change is inevitable.

The crisis of globalization is a unique opportunity for addressing core issues of democracy and human development. It has invigorated a worldwide peoples' movement whose loud demands for change are attracting more and more attention and support: from consumers, environmentalists, trade unionists, women, religious activists, farmers, human rights advocates and ordinary citizens. And those in power are taking note.

At the Asia Pacific Economic Cooperation (APEC) meetings in New Zealand in late 1999 top US trade negotiator Charlene Barshefsky hinted that the single greatest threat to globalization is 'the absence of public support'. Her concerns are justified. There is now a worldwide citizens' movement to rethink the global economy from the ground up. It is a movement which is becoming stronger by the day. And it is premised on one shared and unshakeable central truth. The only way to convince states to act in the interests of their people is to construct a system that will put humans back in control at the center of economic activity.

This final chapter is an attempt to offer concrete steps towards this goal. Tens of thousands of people in dozens of countries around the globe are now working on this project. The following suggestions are rooted in their inspiration and vision.

i Increase citizen participation by revamping the IMF

The global financial system is run by bureaucrats, bankers and mainstream economists. Their decisions have a profound impact on the lives of ordinary people who are never consulted. The institutions which determine global trade and investment policy have an obligation to incorporate the opinions and insights of civil society into their decision-making. The International Monetary Fund (IMF) has been around for more than half a century. In all that time it has still not learned to put people ahead of markets. **Duncan Green** *argues that change is long overdue.*

The annual meeting of the IMF is an extraordinary event, half cult gathering, half beauty contest. The beauty contest takes place in the darkened seminar rooms of the palatial Marriott Hotel in Washington as one Third World official after another steps up to the podium and pitches to the bankers and fund managers who make up the audience. Reforms are on track, they say. We have the political will: inflation is coming down, banks are being overhauled. This is the quest for that elusive beast, 'market confidence'. By publicly swearing fealty to the market, the officials hope to reassure investors and prevent the kind of disastrous capital flight which has brought down economies in Asia, Latin America and Eastern Europe in the last half of the 1990s.

The cult is built on the endless repetition of free-market mantras (liberalize, privatize, encourage foreign trade and transnational corporations) combined with attacks on the cult's enemies – protectionism, government interference, capital controls. One investment banker in a seminar on South Korea adds to the quasi-religious feel by demanding that the government 'respects the sanctity of contracts'. The uniform dark suits and neat haircuts ensure the delegates even look like cult members. After a week of mutual brainwashing, thousands of them emerge blinking into the sticky Washington air, fortified and resolute, and scatter across their globe to continue leading their peoples on the long march towards the market.

In the midst of this talk shop it's easy to forget that the IMF was born with a vision: the creation of a new system to guarantee global economic stability out of the wreckage of depression and World War Two. As initially conceived it was supposed to 'facilitate the expansion and balanced growth of international trade and to contribute thereby to the promotion and maintenance of high levels of employment and real income.' It would oversee a system of fixed exchange rates which would stop countries devaluing to get a competitive edge over their neighbors – a feature of the chaos of the 1930s. It would promote currency convertibility in order to encourage world trade, and it would act as a 'lender of last resort' putting together emergency financing for economies which ran into short-term cash-flow problems.

For 25 years it worked like a dream and the global economy boomed. But then the system collapsed and the 'age of insecurity' began, characterized by wildly fluctuating exchange rates, growing volumes of uncontrolled capital flows and endemic financial instability. Deprived of its role in policing exchange rates, the Fund shifted its focus to the Third World, increasing its emphasis on loans designed to expand the role of market forces in the economies of developing nations.

Today the Fund remains a true believer in the panacea of market forces. It has forced the poorest countries to take their medicine in return for debt relief. In middle-income countries like Korea and Brazil, which have crashed in recent years as the money markets have targeted and destroyed their currencies, the IMF has led the international 'rescue packages'. In return, it has insisted on conditions which include austerity, privatization and structural reforms which try and make over Third World economies along the lines of Anglo-Saxon capitalism. In South Korea in 1998, sacked workers demonstrated with placards saying 'IMFired' and restaurants advertised cut-price 'IMF meals'.

The Asia crash of 1997-98 affected the Fund in contradictory ways. Its experts failed to predict the crash and it now admits making serious mistakes, forcing austerity onto governments when a dose of public spending would have been more appropriate. Such public humiliation has dented the Fund's previously limitless self-belief. Yet the reforms to the 'global financial architecture' which followed the Asia crash have made the agency's influence more pervasive than ever.

So, given its spectacular failures, should the IMF

be abolished? Probably not. And for a couple of good reasons. One is that it would be politically impossible given the current international balance of power. Secondly, in a world of global capital markets some kind of international rules-based institution is required to place checks on the ambitions of the strongest nations. If the IMF did not exist, it would have to be invented.

So what are the alternatives? Could the Fund be turned into a pro-poor, instead of pro-rich, organization? Could it stop obsessing about inflation and return to its original mandate of working for full employment and stability? Or go even further and concentrate on ending poverty and reducing social and economic inequality?

At its 1999 annual meeting the IMF committed itself to poverty reduction for the first time, but critics will need to see what this means in practice. For the organization to become a truly 'pro-poor' institution would require deep changes on a number of broad fronts.

The IMF does not exist in a vacuum. Governments fund it and in return receive votes based on a 'one dollar, one vote' principle – in contrast to the UN's 'one country, one vote' system. As a result, industrialized countries account for over 60 per cent of the voting strength at the IMF and World Bank, compared with just 17 per cent in various UN bodies.

The chief beneficiary is the US which is the only country with a large-enough slice of the votes to enjoy an effective veto of major IMF decisions. That, and the Fund's location in Washington, has helped give the US disproportionate power in using the IMF to pursue its own international agenda.

For example, the IMF rescue package to South Korea in December 1997 included a demand that the country open its market to imports of car parts: hardly crucial to stemming the flow of capital, but a persistent US demand in bilateral trade negotiations for much of the 1990s. One negotiator reportedly told economist Robert Wade that the US had achieved more in six months of crisis bailout talks than in ten years of bilateral trade negotiations.

Steps to reform

A first step in reforming the IMF should be to ensure that its power structure gives a fairer voice to developing countries – especially those most affected by the Fund's operations.

The Fund must also be made more accountable to its members. In the past it has been arrogant and closed to criticism or suggestion. The Fund's negotiators typically arrive in a country with their blueprint for economic reform in their briefcases already drafted, awaiting signature. Only the details are negotiable. It has made some welcome progress in publishing more of its documentation in recent years, but it needs to go further. In its operations overseas, the Fund should consult with social and environmental ministries, parliament and civil society organizations in addition to the ministries of finance. To improve its accountability, it should also be subject to regular external evaluations of its programs and policies.

The IMF must end its love affair with conditionality – Fund-speak for the political and economic conditions attached to its loans. A largely unaccountable body like the IMF should not be telling elected governments how to do their job.

Fund staff have to move beyond their current comfortable circuit of Finance Ministry officials to talk (and listen) to trade unions, peasant organizations, women's groups and non-governmental organizations (NGOs) – the people who will be on the receiving end of the social impact of any agreement. Its programs must reflect more than the concerns of a handful of IMF macro-economists. It should have to convince governments that it is right, rather than coerce them into adopting policies with which they disagree.

The Fund must make improving the lives of ordinary people central to its policies. This may seem obvious. But in practice, its staff often behave as if people were at the service of markets, not the other way round. That still leaves the IMF with an important role in promoting economic stability and low inflation. Boom-bust cycles and escalating prices hurt the poor more than anyone.

But there is no point in achieving low inflation by sacking thousands of workers and cutting health and education services. When an agreement was signed with Nicaragua in 1994, the IMF did just that. It cut thousands of public-sector jobs, froze social spending despite high inflation, introduced fees for health and education and jacked up sales taxes which hit poor people the hardest.

Perhaps more important is the need for a complete change in the organizational culture of the Fund. It must become open to the public, not closed. Pluralist and open-minded, not dogmatic. It must listen, not lecture; and it must learn from its mistakes.

How to achieve that change of heart and mind is a real challenge. Maybe staff should be sent for six months to live with the poor in countries affected by their programs. Or maybe their pay should be linked to their success in reducing poverty. A shift in power to the Third World, away from Washington where all decisions are now taken, would help sensitize Fund staff to local realities and reduce the degree of dogma. Till now foreign postings have been seen almost as a punishment. As one European IMF director recently confessed: 'In the old days, when someone was no good, we said "Oh, just send them to Honduras".'

The IMF entered the new millennium at a crossroads. If it continues down the same old road it will be part of the problem, not part of the solution. A dogmatic, deregulating Fund will merely exacerbate the chronic instability and inequality of the global market. A Fund with a renewed moral purpose and democratic mandate could bring those same forces of chaos under control, to the benefit of the majority of the world's citizens.

Duncan Green is a policy analyst for CAFOD, the UK Catholic aid agency.

ii Establish a global financial authority

National governments have lost control of their ability to manage their own economies. The pressures are too great. The world needs a new international regulatory agency to reduce volatility and inefficiency in global financial markets – a Global Central Bank.

At the time of the Bretton Woods meeting over 50 years ago a Global Central Bank was proposed by the British representative John Maynard Keynes as a way of managing both capital flows and trade balances between countries. But the plan was soon lost in a sea of fractious national interests. It's up for debate again and economist Jane D'Arista has been one of its most persuasive advocates. Here are her responses to some key questions:

How much of your proposal for a global central bank, what you call an International Clearing Bank (ICB), is rooted in Keynes' original vision from the 1940s?

The roots are there, definitely. If you study the Bretton Woods proposals you see that what got left out was the 'clearing house' idea and that's what my proposal would reintroduce. An International Clearing Bank wouldn't print its own currency but Keynes' proposal didn't endorse that either. Instead it would issue an international reserve asset. That would make it possible for countries to engage in trade and financial transactions in their own currencies. At the moment the US dollar is effectively used as the international reserve currency.

Why is that such a serious problem?

The dollar has become the main currency of the global economy. And that is fraught with danger. As the central trade currency, the dollar helps reinforce a model of neocolonialism that's already in place.

Take debt for example. Nations create wealth internally but they have to service their external debts in another currency. That means relying on exports to bring in the foreign exchange necessary to service this debt. Which is why debt is such a burden in the global economy. An ICB would allow each country to pay for cross-border transactions in its own currency and so bar speculators from raiding the world's currency reserves. People could then create wealth in their own currencies within their national economy and be able to have equality of interaction with the rest of the world.

What is it that makes this idea so appealing right now?

Export-led growth has come to dominate the global economy. Heavily-indebted countries that can't make payments in their own currencies – and that is the overwhelming majority – have no choice than to focus on exports. Even if they're successful and build their foreign-exchange reserves they often exhaust them defending their currency against speculators.

Countries have national central banks like the Federal Reserve in the US or the Bundesbank in Germany. Would the ICB function in a similar way?

It would be in charge of a payments system like a national central bank but it would be a way of clearing transactions between countries. I'll give you an example. Let's say I buy your magazine and send you a check in American dollars. You would then take my check and deposit it in your local bank which would in turn take the check to the your central bank, the National Bank of Canada.

Your local bank would receive in payment for the check an addition to its 'reserve account' that would allow it to create a deposit for you in Canadian dollars. So you would have received a US dollar check but you'd get paid in Canadian dollars in your bank account. Your central bank now has an addition on both sides of its balance sheet. It has liability to your bank in terms of increased reserves but it's also got this dollar check.

Is this where the central 'clearing house' comes in?

Yes, your central bank would then take the US dollar check to the International Clearing Bank and receive in payment for it a credit to its international reserve account. So on its balance sheet the National Bank of Canada now has more international reserves. The ICB then returns that check to the US central bank, the Federal Reserve, and accepts payment for it by deducting from the Federal Reserve's international reserve account. At that point the Federal Reserve takes the check back to my bank where it's paid for deducting from my bank's reserve account. My bank then cancels the check and returns it to me.

It sounds plausible but is it politically feasible?

Not everyone likes this idea, especially the US financial system whose institutions are the main beneficiaries of the current global system. The whole point is to put the global payments system back in the hands of public institutions, to cut out the international banks and powerful speculators who've been in charge of foreign-currency markets. It's a lucrative game and fortunes have been made. But money games don't do much to promote trade or facilitate long-term investments. Foreign-exchange investment is axiomatically short-term. That instability is part of the current system which is so wrong and so devastating for so many countries. A stable regime of currency relations is the key to reversing the downward spiral of lower wages and the export of goods and capital on ruinous terms.

You've also mentioned the ICB acting as a 'lender of last resort'. How would that differ from the current role of the IMF?

The problem with the IMF is that it finances bailouts with taxpayer funds. The ICB would maintain a balance sheet for each country with assets and liabilities and could fight balance-of-payments problems in several ways. One would be to enforce Keynes' very strong belief that countries with surplus reserves also have a responsibility to revalue their currency. It's not just a question of the weak to the wall. Let's assume that ICB members agreed that a month should pass before reviewing trade imbalances. That's fine. At the end of the month, if my reserves are five per cent less than yours and yours are five per cent higher than they were before, then we need to revalue and change the currencies. This one month, given that the values of currencies now are shifting on a second-by-second basis, gives the export sectors of all countries a breathing space. They don't have to have such large derivatives contracts and futures contracts on currencies.

On the other hand, let's say after the earthquake in Taiwan the country had to make a lot of payments to buy relief supplies which resulted in an enormous trade imbalance and foreign reserves were draining away. ICB members could say: 'Let's make an adjustment but let's not devalue Taiwan's currency so it has to pay even more for imports.' Instead the ICB could buy from Taiwan's National Central Bank more government securities which would allow it to increase the country's international 'reserve account'. The exchange rate could remain the same, thus not adding financial chaos to natural disaster.

Ultimately, as a lender of last resort the ICB could come to Taiwan and buy from its citizens' holdings of Taiwanese government debt, which would be paid for through the Taiwanese Central Bank by an addition to its international 'reserve account'.

What about the issue of 'governance'? How would an International Clearing Bank be run? And by whom?

The global economy has been run by oligarchs. So how do you make the system more democratic? My thought is that population as well as economic output would determine the voting power of nations participating in an ICB. There would be a rotating

Governing Board composed of representatives from countries that together make up 60 per cent of the global wealth and 60 per cent of the global population. To guard against the ICB becoming a clubhouse for creditors or élites, member central banks would be required to demonstrate genuine accountability to citizens in their own countries. The ICB itself would adhere to tough disclosure and reporting standards. It would have offices in every major financial center and there would be advisory boards from citizens movements and other interest groups outside the financial and government sectors.

The global money managers, the IMF, central bankers and others have put all their faith in market solutions. How do you penetrate that ideology?

Selling an idea like this is politically difficult, even in the NGO community. But I believe things are changing slowly and a fundamental questioning of the current model is now taking place. There are chinks in the armor and we have to be ready to exploit them and explain our vision of what could be different.

In the five years I've been talking to NGOs about this there's been a growing awareness that the private international financial system is the pivotal point. It's that which is driving national governments which are in turn driving the Bretton Woods institutions.

As the world gets more interdependent the systemic crisis and contagion could actually impact on the G7 group of rich countries. It's getting closer. As the public begins to realize that the people running the global economy represent a narrow élite, pressure for change will continue to grow.

Jane D'Arista teaches at Boston University School of Law and is Director of Programs at the Financial Markets Center in Virginia.

iii Honor the Earth

*Global environment standards must be set by a new world body under the mandate of the UN – a Global Environment Organization. These standards must be based on sustainability, equity and justice and should be imbedded in all international trade and investment agreements. 'Trade now, pay later' is the credo of the World Trade Organization (WTO). But take heart. **Steven Shrybman** argues that environmentalists looking for a global system of rules to prevent ecological destruction have much to learn from such a powerful opponent.*

In 1995 more than one hundred nations endorsed an agreement that will have profound impacts on biodiversity, climate change and virtually every other major environmental issue. The agreement is binding and is armed with powerful enforcement measures to ensure that every member lives up to its obligations under the treaty.

The bad news is that this international treaty will be an environmental disaster.

Can't guess which agreement this is? Here are more clues. The treaty wasn't established under the UN Environment Program (UNEP). In fact, it was the product of highly secretive negotiations conducted by public officials working hand-in-glove with the world's largest corporations. Nor is it explicitly about the environment. In fact the treaty rarely mentions the word and never even refers to biodiversity, climate change or desertification.

This international 'environment' treaty is, of course, the World Trade Organization's General Agreement on Trade and Services (GATS). While its proponents deny that it is anything more than a commercial agreement, their protests betray the dangerously myopic perspective they bring to economic and trade policy. The WTO's environmental relevance has also been obscured behind a smoke-screen of jargon. In 'trade-speak' environmental standards become 'technical barriers to trade', food-safety regulations are 'sanitary and phytosanitary measures' while the genetic commons becomes a system of 'intellectual property rights'. This also explains why its backers have been successful in denying the link between trade agreements and environmental concerns.

In broad terms, the WTO is designed to entrench 'grow-now, pay-later' globalization by removing the power of governments to regulate corporate activity in the public interest. The result is that it will undermine our capacity to redirect current economic, development and trade policies towards a truly sustainable path.

Clear evidence of its impact can be seen in a number of successful trade challenges to environmental, conservation and food-safety regulations. Since the WTO was founded four years ago we have watched (its rules prohibit public participation) as the treaty's enforcement machinery has been wheeled into action to punish governments that flout its rules. The growing list of casualties now includes European and Japanese food-safety measures, US clean-air regulations and marine mammal conservation laws, aid and development treaties between Europe and a few impoverished former colonies, and Canadian cultural programs. And the list is likely to grow.

These trade disputes represent only the most visible conflicts between free-trade rules and the environment. Indeed, the most damaging effects of this new global regime occur out of sight, as governments quietly abandon environmental, conservation, worker and consumer protections rather than become embroiled in international trade disputes.

Lately, many environmentalists have come to realize that while they were plodding down the hallways of conference centers trying to negotiate international agreements to combat climate change, protect biodiversity or reduce hazardous-waste trade to poor nations, the ink was drying on an agreement that would only heap fuel on these ecological fires.

This is discouraging, but it is also instructive. The WTO's authority depends on powerful enforcement machinery and in this regard it offers a model for environmental treaties. It proves that when governments are motivated they will sign on to truly binding international agreements.

Any government that violates WTO rules is vulnerable to sanctions – often too severe for even the wealthiest nation to ignore. In the organization's first trade complaint (a challenge by foreign gasoline refiners to US Clean Air Act regulations) the Environmental Protection Agency was given two options. Either remove the offending statute or face trade sanctions in the order of $150 million a year.

A similar fate befell European food-safety regulations last year when the WTO ruled that a European Community (EC) ban on hormone-treated beef violated several rules. The Organization ordered the EC to remove its import controls and, when it refused, authorized trade sanctions worth more than $125 million as the price of its defiance. Moreover, sanctions can be imposed against unrelated products – wherever they will be felt most.

In addition, WTO cases are routinely heard, decided, appealed and resolved within a year. It would be impossible to find any other legal sanctions against government initiatives that are as quick and effective as these. In contrast, international environmental agreements rarely use trade sanctions. Even where they do exist they represent only a pale imitation of the powerful enforcement regime built into the WTO.

Agreements like the Framework Convention on Climate Change and the Biodiversity Convention don't include any enforcement mechanism other than moral persuasion. This lack of teeth explains why governments have so resolutely ignored commitments they made when they signed these agreements at the UN's Earth Summit in Rio back in 1992.

Ultimately, nation states must face legally binding obligations if international environmental goals are to be met. This is where we need to tear several pages from the WTO text concerning enforcement.

Consider, for example, the enforcement provisions of the WTO Agreement on Intellectual Property Rights which were written to promote the interests of global pharmaceutical, biotechnology and media firms. Then imagine environmental goals being taken as seriously as patent rights. If the WTO were transformed into an organization that was as concerned about climate change as it is about the growth of transnational drug companies, we could have an Agreement on Trade-Related Measures To Combat Global Warming. Such an Agreement could require all WTO members to:

- adopt domestic laws to stabilize greenhouse-gas emissions at 1990 levels.
- provide for customs inspection, seizure and disposal of goods that were produced in ways that violate the Agreement.
- establish criminal sanctions for any breach of the legislation or regulations mandated by the Agreement.
- authorize the use of trade sanctions, including cross-retaliatory measures – such as prohibiting the export of energy or energy products – against any jurisdiction that was in breach of its obligations under the Agreement.

It is a measure of how much work lies ahead that a proposal to treat climate change as seriously as pharmaceutical patents would no doubt be greeted with complete incredulity by the WTO. That's why it's critical that governments be pressed to explain why they consider patent protection a higher priority than global warming or biodiversity loss.

But what then do we do with trade and investment deals that are currently exacerbating ecological crises? Does the WTO need to be fundamentally overhauled? Or do proposals to delegate environmental issues to a new UN organization, such as a Global Environmental Organization, make sense?

The answer depends on whether you believe that the environment can be isolated and protected from the main thrust of free-trade policies. In fact, they are cut from the same cloth.

As conflicts between environmental and trade policy became too obvious to deny, free-traders have pushed the environment debate to the margins within the WTO or isolated it entirely.

Current WTO head Michael Moore suggests that environmental issues don't belong in his agency and should be left to 'specialized institutions' with the expertise to address them. He is hoping that most people won't appreciate how intimately interrelated trade and environmental issues really are.

Of course we do need to strengthen the mandates of the international environmental institutions. But it is naïve to imagine that this can happen outside the framework of international economic relations. Indeed, the isolation of these organizations from UN agencies like the World Bank and the WTO explains the marginal influence they have had.

The WTO is as much an environmental agreement as the Basel Convention on Transboundary Waste Shipments is a trade agreement. The distinction is artificial and serves only to defeat efforts to build a sustainable and integrated model for human development.

Trade agreements must serve the goals of combating climate change, preserving biodiversity, assuring food security and protecting diversity. By the same token, international environmental agreements must integrate economic and environmental strategies if they are to be effective and durable.

The need for fundamental reform of the WTO is undeniable. But a supranational Global Environment

Organization (GEO) could also play a supportive role by legitimizing the use of trade and economic sanctions. A GEO will have to be equipped with enforcement mechanisms very much like those of the WTO. Noncompliance would be greeted with sanctions every bit as certain, swift and substantial as those meted out by the WTO. Economic and trade sanctions might not always be necessary, but they'd have to be available just in case.

It is unlikely that Michael Moore can imagine a GEO to rival the power and influence of the WTO he now heads. Indeed, the challenge of establishing an effective international environmental regime will be no less daunting than transforming the WTO. Ultimately, this is because both agendas have precisely the same end point – a treaty to promote ecological and economic security for all peoples, rather than some grotesque notion of international trade built on perpetual growth.

Steven Shrybman works with the West Coast Environmental Law Association in Vancouver and is author of the *Citizen's Guide to the World Trade Organization.*

iv Stop speculation by supporting a 'Tobin Tax' on international financial transactions

Unregulated investment has turned the global economy into a casino where speculators search for instant profits, and damn the consequences! A tax on financial speculation that would put people ahead of profits is urgently needed. **Robin Round** *explains how a tax on financial speculation could help stabilize global markets and capture much-needed funds for global development.*

The world of international finance has become a global casino where investors seeking quick profits bet huge sums around the clock. Unlike investments in goods or services, speculators make money from money alone. No jobs are created, no services provided, no factories built and no widgets produced.

Investors play the bond and currency markets profiting from the minute-to-minute, hourly or daily fluctuations in prices around the world. And the game is big – $1.5 trillion ($1,500,000,000,000) is traded every day, 95 per cent of which is bet on whether currency values and interest rates will rise or fall. Traders make money either way and they thrive when markets are highly unstable, as they were in Southeast Asia in 1997. International investment banks are the big winners, but the game has devastating and far-reaching impacts on the losers. As the Mexican, Southeast Asian, Russian and Brazilian financial crises demonstrated, an enormous human toll is extracted from the citizens of these countries when investors panic and run for the exits. As the economies of nations become increasingly liberalized and integrated, future financial crises are inevitable unless changes are made.

What is the Tobin Tax?

In 1978 Nobel Prize-winning economist James Tobin proposed that a small worldwide tariff (less than half of one per cent) be levied by all major countries on foreign-exchange transactions in order to 'throw some sand in the wheels' of speculative flows. For a currency transaction to be profitable, the change in value of the currency must be greater than the proposed tax. Since speculative currency trades occur on much smaller margins, the Tobin Tax would reduce or eliminate the profits and, logically, the incentive to speculate. The tax is designed to help stabilize exchange rates by reducing the volume of speculation. And it is set deliberately low so as not to have an adverse effect on trade in goods and services or long-term investments.

How would a Tobin Tax benefit the global economy?

It could boost world trade by helping to stabilize exchange rates. Wildly fluctuating rates play havoc with businesses dependent on foreign exchange as prices and profits move up and down, depending on the relative value of the currencies being used. When importers and exporters can't be certain from one day to the next what their money is worth, economic planning – including job creation – goes out of the window. Reduced exchange-rate volatility means that businesses would need to spend less money 'hedging' (buying currencies in anticipation of future price changes), thus freeing up capital for investment in new production.

Tobin's proposed tax would not have stopped the crisis in Southeast Asia, but it could help prevent future crises by reducing overall speculative volume and the volatility that feeds speculative attack.

In what way would the Tobin Tax benefit national governments?

It is designed to reduce the power financial markets have to determine the economic policies of national governments. Traditionally, a country's central bank buys and sells its own currency on international markets to keep its value relatively stable. The bank buys back its currency when a 'glut' caused by an investor sell-off threatens to reduce the currency's value. In the past, most central banks had enough cash in reserve to offset any sell-off or 'attack'.

Not any longer. Speculators now have more cash than all the world's central banks put together. Official global reserves are less than half the value of one day of global foreign-exchange turnover. Many countries are simply unable to protect their currencies from speculative attack.

By cutting down on the overall volume of foreign-exchange transactions, a Tobin Tax would mean that central banks would not need as much reserve money to defend their currency. The tax would allow governments the freedom to act in the best interests of their own economic development, rather than being forced to shape fiscal and monetary policies according to demands of fickle financial markets.

How would the Tobin Tax benefit people?

By making crises less likely, the tax would help avoid the social devastation that occurs in the wake of a financial crisis. It could also be a significant source of global revenue at a time when foreign aid is decreasing and strong domestic anti-tax sentiments are reducing the ability of governments to raise revenue. In the face of increasing income disparity and social inequity, the Tobin Tax represents a rare opportunity to capture the enormous wealth of an untaxed sector and redirect it towards the public good.

Conservative estimates show the tax could yield from $150-300 billion annually. The UN estimates that the cost of wiping out the worst forms of poverty and environmental destruction globally would be around $225 billion per year.

Who will be taxed?

The majority of foreign-exchange dealing is by 100 of the world's largest banks. The top ten control 52 per cent of the market and are mostly American, German and British. Citibank tops the list with a 7.75-per-cent market share and a 1998 volume of foreign exchange transactions which, at $8.5 trillion, exceeded the GDP of the US. These banks operate in their own interest and on behalf of large corporate and private investors, insurance companies, hedge funds, mutual funds and pension funds.

What will be taxed?

Only specialized financial transactions known as 'spots', 'swaps', 'futures' and 'forwards' will be taxed. With the exception of spot transactions, these instruments are known as 'derivatives' because their value is derived from the value of an underlying asset which is not bought or sold in the transaction.

Tourists exchanging dollars to pay for their holidays abroad would not be subject to a Tobin Tax. Debate continues as to whether the tax should apply to any transaction less than a million dollars.

How does the Tobin Tax work?

The tax would target only speculative currency transactions. Because it is not easy to determine which types of transactions are speculative and which are associated with legitimate trade in goods and services, the tax hinges on the speed of a transaction. Speed is the primary difference between speculative and legitimate trade. Productive investment works on the medium to long term while speculators flip investments like pancakes, profiting by the daily, hourly and minute-to-minute fluctuations in interest rates and currency values. Eighty per cent of all speculative transactions occur within seven days or less – 40 per cent occur in two days or less.

A Tobin Tax would automatically penalize short-term exchanges, while barely affecting the incentives for commodity trading and long-term capital investments.

Won't speculators find ways to evade the tax?

Inevitably. However, this has never dissuaded governments from collecting taxes, particularly 'sin taxes' designed to stem unacceptable behavior. The real question is, how do you minimize evasion?

A Tobin Tax could be difficult to evade. Because currency transactions are tracked electronically, in theory the tax would be easy to collect through the computer systems that record each trade. While the amount of money is enormous, the number of centers where trading occurs and the number of traders is not. Eighty per cent of foreign-exchange trading takes place in just seven cities. Agreement by London, New York and Tokyo alone would capture 68 per cent of speculative trading.

Won't speculators shift operations to offshore tax havens?

Agreement between nations could help avoid the relocation threat, particularly if the tax were charged at the site where payments are settled or 'netted'. Globally, the move towards a centralized settlement system means transactions are being tracked by fewer and fewer institutions. Hiding trades is becoming increasingly difficult. Transfers to tax havens like the Cayman Islands could be penalized at double the agreed rate or more.

What is the biggest barrier to the Tobin Tax?

It's not technical or administrative. It's political. The tax is seen as a threat by the financial community and has met with stiff resistance by a sector with massive political clout. The very idea of putting people ahead of markets challenges the foundations of the current global economic model and those who control it.

Can the opposition be overcome?

In the wake of recent global financial crises governments everywhere are examining their faith in free markets. Even the World Bank and the International Monetary Fund praised Malaysia's use of capital controls to jump-start its battered economy in 1997-8. This is a fundamental shift in attitude, unimaginable until recently.

The political appeal of this tax to cash-strapped governments and multilateral agencies worldwide can't be underestimated. At the UN Social Summit +5 in Geneva in June 2000, 160 governments agreed to conduct a rigorous analysis on new and innovative sources of funding for social development, including a currency transaction tax. NGOs from around the world fought hard for this crucial study and believe it will make a significant contribution to the intergovernmental debate on a Tobin Tax.

Who supports the Tobin Tax?

The international trade union movement, the Canadian Parliament, the Finnish Government and a growing number of academics and elected representatives all support the tax. The European Parliament, and parliamentarians in the UK and France have held debates on the Tobin proposal and groups of parliamentarians are active in Brazil and throughout Europe. Over 400 parliamentarians from 21 countries have signed a World Parliamentarians Call for a Tobin Tax and 160 economists from 29 countries signed a similar appeal launched in June 2000. Citizens' movements for a Tobin Tax are active around the world. These include: CIDSE in Europe, the Halifax Initiative in Canada, KEPA in Finland, War on Want in Britain, ATTAC in France and Brazil, CCEJ in Korea and the Tobin Tax Initiative in the US. These and other groups have established the International Tobin Tax Network to share information and coordinate actions as they work to build public and political support for the tax.

This is only one aspect of the fundamental reform of the global financial system and is not a panacea for the world's financial ills and development woes. The democratization of economic decision-making and the equitable redistribution of wealth must become the central principles upon which governments act in the new millennium.

The real work has just begun. Citizens and politicians around the world must not let the powerful forces who oppose the Tobin Tax stifle, manipulate and ultimately undermine an essential public debate on controlling global financial markets.

The Tobin Tax deserves a fair hearing. Only widespread popular support and public pressure can ensure it.

Robin Round directs the Tobin Tax campaign of the Halifax Initiative, a coalition of Canadian NGOs.

v Control capital for the public good

New global investment rules hammered out at the World Trade Organization and entrenched in regional trading treaties like the North American Free Trade Agreement (NAFTA) give carte blanche to wealthy investors while demanding nothing in return. An alternative investment code is needed for democratic control of capital and to *stimulate investment that benefits local communities. **Tony Clarke** argues that corporations have a debt to all of us. He suggests an Alternative Investment Treaty for bringing the rule of law to big business.*

When negotiations for a Multilateral Agreement on Investment (MAI) began to fall apart in the Spring of 1998 pundits and journalists took stock of the international citizens campaign that had turned the tables on the architects of economic globalization.

Britain's venerable *Financial Times* (FT) referred to the final scene from the movie Butch Cassidy and the Sundance Kid when the two amiable but confused American crooks wind up in Latin America facing the Bolivian military. The FT used the scene to portray the bewilderment which overcame Western leaders as the MAI unraveled.

'Picture a group of politicians and diplomats looking over their shoulders at an encroaching horde of vigilantes whose motives and methods are only dimly understood in most national capitals, asking despairingly: "Who are these guys?"'

Praising the effectiveness of the anti-MAI campaign, one veteran trade diplomat said: 'This episode is a turning point. It means we have to rethink our approach to international economic and trade negotiations.'

A rethink is certainly overdue. But it may come as a surprise to the MAI's well-heeled backers that the deal's critics were not flatly opposed to the idea of a global investment treaty. Instead, many anti-MAI campaigners insisted that a totally different kind of global treaty was needed – one that would bring transnational corporations (TNCs) under the rule of law rather than provide them with a bill of rights and freedoms, as the MAI did.

So how do we begin to construct an alternative framework which is so fundamentally at odds with the current neo-liberal orthodoxy?

The first step is to review the basic goals of investment. Capital needs to be seen primarily as an instrument or means of development not as tool for turning a quick profit at the expense of people and the Earth. Specifically, investment should serve the priorities of just and sustainable development. Nor is this just pie-in-the-sky. The building blocks have already been laid in numerous covenants and charters of the United Nations.

Take the 1948 Universal Declaration of Human Rights and its accompanying Covenant on Economic, Social and Cultural Rights; or the UN Covenant on Civil and Political Rights. Together they assert the supremacy of democratic rights and freedoms over political and economic tyranny. These covenants have been reinforced by more recent charters from the Rio Summit on the Environment, the Beijing Summit on Women and the Copenhagen Summit on Social Development.

What's more, the 1974 UN Charter on the Economic Rights and Duties of States recognized the responsibilities of national governments to regulate foreign investment in order to serve the economic, social and environmental priorities of development. At the center of this Charter is the principle that capital has 'social obligations'.

This means that capital formation is a social process built on present and previous generations of human labor. Businesses use both economic and social infrastructure, things like roads and bridges and services like public education, sanitation and clean water. They also make use of natural resources extracted from the Earth for energy and production. For these reasons there is both a social and an ecological mortgage on all capital – corporations have a debt to pay back to both society and nature. This 'stored value' of capital provides legitimate grounds for putting obligations on investors.

Such a reassessment won't happen without changing both the venue and process of negotiations. As a rich-nations club where most of the 'Global Fortune 500' – the biggest and wealthiest corporations – are based, the Organization for Economic Cooperation and Development (OECD) is not the place to construct an alternative treaty along these lines. Nor is the World Trade Organization (WTO). Although the WTO includes most of the world's nation states, its power structure is heavily weighted against the developing countries.

The only appropriate place is the UN itself. Despite disturbing signs of corporate infiltration in UN affairs, the foundation for developing an alternative framework is located there, along with more equitable decision-making. What is required is leadership within UN circles to kick-start the process.

The main principles of an Alternative Investment Treaty should include:

• **Citizens' rights** – Investment should be designed to ensure that capital serves the basic rights and needs of all citizens including: human rights (adequate food, clothing, shelter); social rights (quality health care, education, social services); labor rights (employment, fair wages, unions, health and safety standards); environmental rights (protection of air, waters, forests, fish, wildlife and nonrenewable resources) and cultural rights (preservation of peoples' identity, values, customs, heritage).

• **State responsibilities** – To ensure that citizens' rights are respected governments have the right and responsibility to regulate the national economy. These powers should include the right to protect strategic areas of their economies (finance, energy, communications) by establishing public enterprises. And the right to protect sensitive areas known as the 'commons' (the environment, health care, culture) through government-run public services.

• **Corporate obligations** – Although foreign-based corporations can expect fair treatment and a reasonable return on investment (compensation for expropriation of assets) they must maintain certain social obligations such as performance standards designed to ensure citizens' basic needs and rights. They must also recognize that governments have the right to protect and enhance strategic areas of their economies and the 'commons'. And they must contribute a portion of their capital to the 'commons' by paying their fair share of taxes.

An Alternative Investment Treaty based on these fundamental principles would include the following key elements:

• **Fair treatment** – Foreign investment would be welcome provided social obligations were met. The concept of 'national treatment', which is used to force governments to treat foreign corporations on the same terms as domestic companies, should be discarded. Instead the 'stored value' of capital would be the basis for establishing obligations for fair treatment of foreign-based corporations.

• **Social obligations** – Governments would have the legal right to require all corporations, both foreign and domestic, to meet basic social obligations such as labor standards, environmental safeguards and social-security contributions.

• **Performance standards** – To ensure that foreign investment serves national-development priorities, governments would be allowed to require standards such as job quotas, balancing imports with exports, quotas on natural-resource exports or restrictions on the repatriation of profits. In return for access to a country's markets and resources, a government could require that a foreign company create a specified number of new jobs in the community or adhere to restrictions on the export of nonrenewable resources. These initiatives are both feasible and practical. Canada's Foreign Investment Review Act once provided the Canadian Government with the policy tools to apply this kind of performance requirement on foreign investments.

• **Investment incentives** – To ensure that corporations keep these social obligations, governments may use investment 'incentives' including: grants, loans and subsidies; procurement practices; tax incentives and limits on profit remittances for foreign companies that fail their social obligations. Governments could decide, for example, to buy from either foreign or domestic companies as a way of attracting productive investment.

• **Public enterprises** – All governments have a responsibility to use tax revenues for protecting the 'commons' through public investments. These could include exercising public ownership over key sectors of the economy; establishing social programs and public services; safeguarding ecologically sensitive areas; and protecting cultural heritage.

• **Expropriation measures** – Fair compensation should be paid to foreign corporations whose physical assets are expropriated for public purposes. But not when social or environmental regulations add to business costs. Compensation should be determined by national law with due regard to the value of the initial investment, the valuation of the properties for tax purposes and the amount of wealth taken out of the country during the period of investment.

So a foreign corporation could not demand compensation for an environmental law that placed a quota on the export of a nonrenewable resource or a health ban on the sale of toxic substances, on the grounds that such measures would reduce the corporation's profit margins. Nor could a foreign company claim compensation for loss of future profits because government actions prevent a planned investment from going ahead.

• **Financial transactions** – All governments have a right to require that foreign investment be used for productive rather than speculative purposes; that foreign corporations deposit a percentage of their profits in the central bank for a specified minimum period; that foreign-exchange transactions be taxed in order to slow down currency speculation. For example, to prevent the sudden exodus of speculative capital from Chile, 'speed bump' measures were introduced which required investment to remain in the country for at least a year.

• **Dispute settlement** – In the event of a dispute citizens, governments and corporations would all have the right to be heard. Disputes filed by citizens would be heard by national courts which would have powers to invoke injunctions and award monetary compensation. Through this process any one of the three parties with legal standing could bring a suit for monetary compensation but not for violation of the investment rules aimed at striking down national laws. To ensure that non-governmental organizations (NGOs), native communities, environment and women's groups, trade unions and others have equal access to the dispute-settlement mechanism, national and international funds should be established for citizen intervenors.

Tony Clarke is Director of the Polaris Institute in Ottawa, Canada and board member of the International Forum on Globalization.

CONTACTS

International

Focus on the Global South
Excellent Bangkok-based research and advocacy group with wide-ranging contacts throughout the South.
CUSRI, Chulalongkorn University, Bagkok 10330, Thailand.
Tel: +66 2 218 7363/4/5
Fax: +66 2 255 9976
Website: www.focusweb.org

International Forum on Globalization
Loose-knit network of anti-globalization NGOs and activists from 40 countries North and South.
1555 Pacific Avenue, San Francisco, CA USA.
Tel: +1 415 771 3394
Fax: +1 415 771 1121
Website: www.ifg.org

Third World Network
Coalition of Southern NGOs with an action, research, publishing focus. Combines powerful analysis with effective international lobbying.
228 McAllister Rd., Penang 10400, Malaysia
Tel: +60 (4) 226 6728
Fax: +60 (4) 226 4505
Website: www.twnside.org

Oxfam International
Poverty action and aid group with wide-ranging concerns, excellent research and strong grassroots experience. With projects in 120 countries and 11 independent national Oxfams. See website for local contact details:
Website:
www.ca.org.au/oxfam/index.html

ATTAC (Association for the Taxation of financial Transactions for the Aid of Citizens)
International group, launched in France in 1998, campaigning for international tax on currency speculation and roll-back of neo-liberal economic agenda.
See website for local contacts and complete information.
Website: www.attac.org/

Aotearoa / New Zealand

Jubilee 2000/Debt Action Network
Member of church-based international movement to cancel Third World debt.
C/o CWS, PO Box 22-652, Christchurch
Tel: +64 (3) 366 9274
Fax: +64 (3) 365 2919

Australia

Australian Council for Overseas Aid
Coalition representing broad spectrum of NGOs campaigning on global speculation tax and unjust world economic order.
14 Napier Close, Deakin, ACT 2600
Tel: +61 (2) 6285 1816
Fax: +61 (2) 6285 1720
Website: www.acfoa.asn.au

Canada

Council of Canadians
Nationwide membership organization campaigning on issues of national sovereignty and against corporate globalization and free trade.
904-251 Laurier St West, Ottawa, ON K1P 5J6
Tel: +1 613 233 2773
Fax: +1 613 233 6776
Website: www.canadians.org

Contacts

Halifax Initiative
NGO coalition campaigning for global tax on foreign exchange transactions and financial speculation.
1 Nicholas St., Suite 412, Ottawa, ON K1N 7B7
Tel: +1 613 789 4447
Fax: +1 613 241 2292
Website:
www.sierraclub.ca/national/halifax

Canadian Centre for Policy Alternatives
Independent policy research institute with activist stance. Publishes on wide range of globalization issues including free trade and corporate agenda.
#410-75 Albert Street, Ottawa, ON K1P 5E7
Tel: +1 613 563 1341
Fax: +1 613 233 1458
Website: www.policyalternatives.ca

UK

World Development Movement
Education and campaigning organization focusing on UK foreign policy, Third World debt and globalization.
25 Beehive Pl., London SW9 SQ4
Tel: +44 207 737 6215
Fax: +44 207 274 8232
Website: www.wdm.org

War on Want
Activist group campaigning for global currency transation tax.
Fenner Brockway House,
37-39 Great Guildford St.,
London SE1 0ES
Tel: +44 207 620 1111
Fax: +44 207 261 9291
Website: www.wow@gn.apc.org

USA

Institute for Food and Development Policy (Food First)
Long-established research and advocacy group focusing on food and agricultural policy, poverty and globalization.
398 60th St., Oakland, CA 94618
Tel: +1 510 654 4400
Fax: +1 510 654 4551
Website: www.foodfirst.org

50 Years Is Enough Network
Coalition of citizen's groups aiming to reform and/or dismantle the IMF, the World Bank and the WTO, with links to similar groups internationally.
1247 E St, SE, Washington, DC 20003
Tel: +1 202 463 2265
Fax: +1 202 544 9359
Website: www.50years.org

Institute for Trade and Agricultural Policy
Anti-globalization research and strategy building around sustainable agriculture and trade policy.
2105 First Ave South, Minneapolis, MN 55404
Tel: +1 612 870 3400
Fax: +1 612 870 4846
Website: www.iatp.org

Public Citizen/Global Trade Watch
Critical analysis of corporate-led globalization combined with education and lobbying on reforms to global economic structures and US economic policies.
215 Pennsylvania Ave SE, Washington, DC 20001
Tel: +1 202 588 1000
Fax: +1 202 547 7392
Website: www.citizen.org

Bibliography

False Dawn: the delusions of global capitalism, John Gray (Granta Books, London, 1998)

For the Common Good, Herman E Daly and John B Cobb Jr, (Beacon Press, Boston, 1989)

Human Development Report 1999 (Globalization with a human face), UN Development Program (OUP, New York, 1999)

Jihad vs McWorld, Benjamin R Barber (Ballantine Books, New York, 1995)

MAI: Round 2, Tony Clarke & Maude Barlow (Stoddard Publishing, Toronto, 1998)

Our Ecological Footprint, Mathis Wackernagel and William Rees (New Society Press, Gabriola Island, BC, 1997)

Panic Rules. Everything you need to know about the global economy, Robin Hahnel (South End Press, Cambridge, MA 1999)

Taming Global Finance: a better architecture for growth and equity, Robert Blecker (Economic Policy Institute, Washington, 1999)

The Cancer Stage of Capitalism, John McMurtry (Pluto Press, London, 1999)

The Conquest of Paradise, Kirkpatrick Sale (Knopf, New York, 1990)

The Crisis of Global Capitalism, George Soros (Perseus Books, 1998)

The Post-Corporate World: life after capitalism, David Korten (Kumarian and Berrett-Koehler, San Francisco, CA and West Hartford, CT 1999)

Unequal Freedoms: The global market as an ethical system, John McMurtry (Garamond, Toronto, ON and Kumarian, West Hartfort, CT 1998)

Your Money or Your Life! the tyranny of global finance, Eric Toussaint (Pluto Press, London, 1999)

Periodicals/Papers

Economic Justice Report, Ecumenical Coalition for Economic Justice, 947 Queen St E, Ste 208, Toronto, ON Canada M4M 1J9

Dollars and Sense, One Summer St, Somerville, MA 02143, USA

CCPA Monitor, #410 - 75 Albert St, Ottawa, ON K1P 5E7, Canada

Multinational Monitor, 1530 P St., NW, Washington, DC, USA 20005

'Globalization and Employment', Panos Briefing No 33, London, May 1999

'Globalization for Whom?', Mark Weisbrot, Preamble Center, Washington DC, 1998

'Economic Sovereignty in a Globalizing World', framework paper for global financial architecture, Walden Bello, Kamal Malhotra, Nicola Bullard, Marco Mezzera, Bangkok 1999

The New Internationalist **www.newint.org**

Index

Index